EBURY PRESS

THE URBAN ELITE V. UNION OF INDIA

Rohin Bhatt is a queer, non-binary lawyer who practices in the Supreme Court. Their work has spanned not just activism inside the courtroom but also outside it. They write extensively on issues of queer rights and human rights.

ADVANCE PRAISE FOR THE BOOK

'Across nations, the LGBTQIA+ movement has been one of the most formidable campaigners for human rights. Their quest for equality in India will of course meet with success in our time; Bhatt walks us expertly through the battles of the present'

—**Aakar Patel, chair, Amnesty International India**

'For three decades, the battle for queer rights has unfolded in India's courts. *The Urban Elite v. Union of India* offers critical insights into the latest chapter of this struggle—marriage equality. This book is a call to action, urging us to turn judicial setbacks into stronger, more resilient political movements for the future'

—**Anish Gawande, national spokesperson, Nationalist Congress Party (Sharadchandra Pawar)**

'This book is a passionate and loving celebration of the journey through its successes and setbacks for the right to equality of the LGBT community. The re-creation of arguments in the courtroom surpasses anything we have seen in live-streaming. It ends on a note of hope, reinforcing my belief that there will always be a stream of resistance from marginalized communities in constitutional courts, which till recently were out of bounds for them'

—**Indira Jaising, senior advocate, Supreme Court of India**

'A searing chronicle of a case, the state of the LGBTQIA movement and a deeply personal journey. With this book, Bhatt has claimed his space as a leading voice for the queer community'

—**Saurabh Kirpal, senior advocate, Delhi High Court**

the
urban elite
v.
Union of India

THE UNFULFILLED CONSTITUTIONAL
PROMISE OF MARRIAGE (IN)EQUALITY

ROHIN BHATT

EBURY
PRESS

An imprint of Penguin Random House

EBURY PRESS

Ebury Press is an imprint of the Penguin Random House group of
companies whose addresses can be found at global.penguinrandomhouse.com

Published by Penguin Random House India Pvt. Ltd
4th Floor, Capital Tower 1, MG Road,
Gurugram 122 002, Haryana, India

Penguin
Random House
India

First published in Ebury Press by Penguin Random House India 2024

10 9 8 7 6 5 4 3 2 1

The views and opinions expressed in this book are the author's own and the
facts are as reported by them which have been verified to the extent possible,
and the publishers are not in any way liable for the same.

Please note that no part of this book may be used or reproduced in any manner
for the purpose of training artificial intelligence technologies or systems.

ISBN 9780143467564

Typeset in Goudy Old Style by MAP Systems, Bengaluru, India
Printed at Replika Press Pvt. Ltd, India

www.penguin.co.in

MIX
Paper | Supporting
responsible forestry
FSC™ C016779

To the strong women in my life,

Mukta baa, my grandmother, and the love of my life

Mum, who has always been my strongest advocate

Panistha, my best friend and my worst enemy

Contents

Foreword

What happens to a lawyer when he is invested in a case personally but represents another person of his ilk? I must admit that in many of the cases that I have handled as a lawyer, I have been invested so much that I felt as if the cases were my own. However, when I went to sleep, I knew that I was dealing with another person's case. That was a source of comfort.

Rohin, on the other hand, was the one eating, breathing and sleeping the case, as it were. Though he appeared as a lawyer and my assisting junior in the same-sex marriage case, Supriyo Chakraborty v. Union of India, he knew that the case affected him and all others of alternative sexuality. That is partly what this book is about.

From being nearly arrested for merely loving, to the emotions that ran through him when the Supreme Court pronounced the verdict in *Supriyo Chakraborty*, one can feel his sentiment. When he describes his emotions on the Solicitor General taunting, '*There is no stigma*,' when referring to the lives of the queer people in the post-Navtej era, you feel one with him. When he says how *Supriyo Chakraborty* was '*a judicial punch in the gut of queer movement*', you feel the punch yourself.

But the book is also about much more. Apart from charting out the history of Section 377 of the Indian Penal Code, via *Naz Foundation*, *Suresh Kumar Koushal*, *NALSA* and *Navtej Johar* in and out of court, it describes in detail the arguments presented by the petitioners, the replies by the respondents and the rejoinder by the petitioners on a day-to-day basis in the Supreme Court. The reader gets a ringside view of the case, not in technical legalese but in an easy-to-comprehend language. The exchanges between the bench and bar and between the counsel of the competing parties are penned in detail. Rohin can communicate complex legal concepts in simple language. This is the cornerstone of the book and will be handy for those who want to critique *Supriyo Chakraborty*.

Rohin has interspersed the book with anecdotes from his own life that lay out the rich tapestry of his experience and qualify him to deal with the issues in the book in both objective and subjective manners. Though he is only twenty-six years of age, an ordinary reader would be amazed at the experiences Rohin speaks of, which exhibit his maturity in dealing with a very difficult subject.

He deals with the judgment in *Supriyo Chakraborty* not only in emotional terms but objectively, with fault lines of each judgment, including the failure of the court to recognize the right to marry, contrary to its earlier rulings, where it has held that there is indeed a right to marry; reading of the terms, 'husband' and 'wife' in the Special Marriage Act in gender neutral manner; on whether queer couples could adopt; on queer couples' legal pathways to be protected from violence, etc.

He also points to the case of a gay couple in Kerala, one of whom died. Even though the family disowned him, the Kerala High Court held that the family alone had the right to his bodily remains and were indeed handed over the body. The lover, on the other hand, *'had merely been left out in the cold winds of exclusion and homophobia'*, typifying the extant reality of the LGBTQIA+ movement.

He rightly ends with a discussion around the issue, 'How does one chart the way forward for the queer movement?'

I will not let you in on his answers. For that, you must read the book. Imbued with the passion of a young activist lawyer, this book is eminently readable, for the lay and the initiated readers alike. It is worth every rupee that the reader will pay for it. It is one of a kind.

Anand Grover
Senior advocate
Supreme Court of India
August 2024, Delhi

Chapter 1

Queer Revolutions: The Personal, the Political and the Legal[1]

> *'Hope' is the thing with feathers*
> *That perches in the soul*
> *And sings the tune without the words*
> *And never stops—at all.*
> —Emily Dickinson, '"Hope" Is the
> Thing with Feathers'

It was a cold December night in 2017. As a nineteen-year-old, I was enthralled by the promise of Grindr, a gay dating app that I had just stumbled upon. Until I discovered Grindr, the world was a lonely place. I was a nerdy queer child who was bullied and would often look up the word 'homosexual' in the yellowed pages of my mother's copy of the Oxford English Dictionary.

Eventually, I ended up going on one of the first dates with a young doctor. After warming ourselves with several cups of coffee on a chilly winter night in Ahmedabad, we were driving around the city. I do not remember what we were talking animatedly about, but one thing was certain— there was sexual tension, the kind that makes your heart beat so loud that the other person can almost hear it. I think they felt it too, for they leaned in and kissed me at a traffic signal. I blushed. Immediately, there was the sound of a police baton on the window.

thud *thud* *thud*

I froze.

A policeman barked at us in Gujarati, 'Bahar nikdo gaadi ma thi' (Get out of the car.) He told us he would call our parents (although we were both adults) and that he was, amongst other things, arresting us under Section 377 of the Indian Penal Code. The reason? I was kissing another man.

Having gone through a fair bit of law school by then, I knew that homosexuality was a crime in India, and that I was an unconvicted felon. A conviction under Section 377 of the Indian Penal Code (IPC), which criminalized homosexuality, carried a term of life imprisonment, or imprisonment upto ten years and also a fine. Not to mention the consequences of a criminal trial, and the social and moral censure that would undoubtedly follow.

I had no idea what to do. I froze. In that moment, my mind raced. I was not out to my parents. To my friends. To the world at large. Hell, if I am being honest, I was not out to myself. What was going to happen? Would I be thrown out of the house? Would the world accept me for who I am? My mind was racing, and my heart was beating at a gazillion beats per second.

After much cajoling, and the person I was with paying a hefty bribe (he refused to let me chip in), the policeman let us go. As I write about that incident today, my hands quiver and my throat goes dry. What happened then was part of the reason I did not come out well until I knew that I had perhaps 'made up' to the world at large for my sexuality. Admission into a master's degree at Harvard Medical School sure ought to compensate for my queerness, right? What I lacked in supposed normativity when it came to sexuality, I 'fixed' by checking another box. I did not have the guts to come out to anyone in person except for my sister and a friend. I mostly did it over text messages. Everyone else came to know about it through an Instagram post on 28 March 2021, a few weeks after I got into Harvard.

As a queer person who is a lawyer, this book is animated by lucid rage at having almost been arrested for merely loving, and an abiding disgruntlement with the Supreme Court for its judgment in Suresh Kumar Koushal and Another v. Naz Foundation & Ors (2013)[2] which recriminalized homosexuality after the Delhi High Court, in Naz Foundation v. Govt of NCT of Delhi (2009),[3] had decriminalized it, and now in Supriyo Chakraborty v. Union of India in October 2023, where the Supreme Court has held that there is no fundamental right to marry, and that the right to marry is a statutory right which queer persons do not have. For me, as it is for other queer persons, the meandering legal path that the queer movement takes, despite all of its internal fractures and divisions, is personal, and the personal is legal. This lattice of this book will mesh the personal with the legal. While it is primarily about the marriage equality litigation, it will intertwine with it my lived experiences of queer joy and euphoria, of homophobia, and of the way I have found myself in the midst of the queer rights movement in India.

* * *

You do not have to be queer or a lawyer to read this book. But it is about queerness and the law. I want to talk about the experience of the law through a lens of queerness, as someone who has been a part of it, not just as a lawyer but also as an activist. This book also maps my short journey as a lawyer. Usually, one does not write such a book until one is either bald and wrinkled, or dying. Well, perhaps this is what it means to be queer. You break norms. You do not adhere to the rules and boundaries which are set for you. *Deviants*. That is what we were called for the longest of times. Perhaps it is time to reclaim the word.

The book is not a legal commentary, nor is it a hyper-technical book on the law. It is not going to be too legalistic but is aimed at breaking down complex court-speak in a way that is accessible to the people who may have not studied the law.

A lot of people were following the marriage equality case which came to be called Supriyo Chakraborty v. Union of India (after the lead petition), along with connected matters where nearly fifty non-heterosexual couples were asking for the right to marry. Since this was one of the first cases that had garnered wide public interest and was being live-streamed, I was asked a number of questions: Was approaching the Supreme Court when the cases were pending before the high court the right move? Why were we seeking a declaration? What is a declaration? What does a mandamus mean? What is constitutional comity? What is the difference between reading down and reading up a provision? But perhaps, the most persistent question was: Will we win? Fascinatingly, whenever the last question was asked, 'we' was used not just by queer people but also by allies. Since the live-streaming had taken the case into living rooms, a lot of people, gay or straight, felt as if they had a personal stake in it.

The idea behind writing this book is to take the legal debates from the cloistered court halls of the constitutional courts of the country into dining rooms and other places where these conversations often take place. Throughout the course of this book, I will be relying on the documents that the petitioners, respondents and intervenors had filed, namely, the petitions, written arguments, counters, affidavits, reports of various bodies, news reports and case laws, etc. in the litigious path of the queer movement. In many ways, this book traces the way love and identity politics around gender and sexuality play out and have played out in court. As a result, it is a ballad that sings of the attempts to undo institutionalized homophobia in our courts, in polity, in policies, in our executive and in our democracy. Much of this work has happened through wielding the Constitution as a charter of rights in courts of law. But it is also an elegy which tells the tale of the harms meted out to queer individuals in the form of medical interventions, state-sanctioned assault by the police, attacks by vigilante groups and corrective rapes by families.

* * *

The book starts on the day of the judgment in Supriyo Chakraborty v. Union of India, or the marriage equality case.[4] The judgment came as a punch in the gut to those of us who were lawyers—during the course of the hearings and considering the tone and tenor of the judges, we knew that we were supposedly asking for too much, but the fact that we did not get anything was shocking. I want to trace the emotions of that day and reflect on what we did right, but also introspect on where we went wrong.

In the second chapter, I will trace the legal history of queerness in India, from precolonial times to the present day. Like most countries that were a part of the British Commonwealth, we incorporated Section 377, an anti-sodomy law, into our penal code. I do want to spend time dissecting the cases and the movements to help you better understand why and how the marriage equality petitions ended up before the Supreme Court.

The third chapter will focus on and briefly analyse the nearly 25,000 pages of material that were submitted to the court by the petitioners and dissect each argument that the petitioners made. This chapter will be dedicated to analysing the first four days of arguments and breaking down the legalese therein.

The fourth chapter will summarize the arguments which were made by the respondents. Like the previous chapter, it will primarily be focused on legal arguments that can be tailored to both legal and non-legal audiences. It will also look at the various steps that the government suggested to derail the hearings.

The fifth chapter will be a brief one—the arguments in rejoinder; how the petitioners responded to the curveballs; the reduction of queer lives into a circus and the arguments of alarm which were played by the respondents.

The final chapter will critique the judgment and trace possibilities for the future. Keeping in mind the judgment as well as sociopolitical developments in the queer rights movement, where do we take the movement once the marriage question is solved? How do we foster a legal culture of inclusivity? Has the Supreme Court been a true ally to queer people? These are a few questions that the chapter will answer.

This book will also attempt to trace the history of the way queer rights were won, are won and perhaps will continue to be won in courts, and will focus on the litigation around marriage equality.

* * *

At the heart of this book, however, is a caveat. We must understand that queer liberation cannot and will not be achieved solely through litigation; revolutions are never won through litigation. Law is as much a tool for oppression and subjugation as it is a tool to protect freedom and liberty. Why then do I find myself in the courts every day? Why do I want to dedicate my life to fighting for social justice and protecting fundamental rights? It is because I believe in the power of the law to be able to effectuate social change when it is combined with the mobilization of a social justice movement. One can win cases and get a favourable judgment after a few days of passionate arguments. But unless this is backed by a social movement to metamorphize the judgment into actionable rights, little can be done.

Take the Navtej Singh Johar judgment, for example. Justice Rohinton Nariman's judgment ordered the State to publicize the judgment and sensitize officials. A set of Right to Information (RTI) applications were filed by Akhilesh Godi, an IITian who was one of the petitioners in the Section 377 case seeking information on whether any progress had been made on the said order. The replies claimed that the files were either lost or the agency had not received any instruction on the same.[5] Issues like this where we have not followed up, to my mind, have been failures where those of us who are queer and legally equipped have failed to hold the government to account. But that is the best-case scenario. There will be times when we lose a case. It is then that the power of social movements becomes essential. Sisterhood, allyship and community become a sine qua non. It becomes important to push back at a wrong law, if a case is lost in the courts. We must then take to the streets, to houses of Parliament, to state legislatures and to policymakers, in school, in families, neighbourhoods and even in workplaces. If we do not do that, then all the efforts will be for naught. We must create an alternate vision that is transformative and inclusive in cases of loss like that in the marriage equality case to disrupt the status quo. We must show how the results arrived at are wrong.

In the Indian politico-legal system, the success of a social justice movement can come in multiple ways. Primary among them is convincing our fellow citizens of the positions we take and then electing our representatives who will then constitute the legislature and pass laws. The second is litigating our rights in court. In this book, on account of the nature of the manner in which queer rights have been achieved, we will focus only on the latter. In any democracy, winning hearts and minds is important, but that does not necessarily mean a law will be passed to reflect such a change.

Consider the Women's Reservation Act of 2023—there is a broad consensus in society on two things, namely, that women are underrepresented in our legislature and that they deserve equal political representation. However, even when corrective action was taken, it was half-hearted.[6] Lawmaking, after all, is the prerogative of Parliament and state legislatures, and seldom do changed societal norms force Parliament to pass a law to reflect them. Nor does the passing of a law necessarily precipitate into actionable rights, as every legal scholar will tell you. But how does anti-majoritarian litigation in courts on the rights of a community that has been criminalized and systematically disenfranchised take place in India? What are the roadblocks? How does one seek to protect these rights? These are a few questions that I seek to address in this book. But I chose to mention the other two ways because this is what the petitioners were told to do in the arguments by those that opposed marriage equality: Marriage is a social institution, and it should be the society and the legislature that take a call about who can marry whom and how.

When the queer community asks our constitutional courts, namely the high courts and the Supreme Court to strike down laws like the Telangana Eunuchs Act[7] or Section 377 (both of which have been struck down), which were used in colonial times to stigmatize queer persons, treating queerness as unpalatable and as outside the conversations of polite society, we do it because we believe in the approach to participate equally in society, to avoid condemnation as if we were a contamination. This was because we believe in legal victories more in this post-Navtej era. Convincing the courts that legislations which discriminate are arbitrary, brazenly unconstitutional and fall foul of the constitutional guarantee of equality is perhaps easy. Winning cases is easier than winning hearts and minds—it perhaps forces people to acknowledge that we have a claim to equal citizenship, and that since the judgements of the court are binding, there is little they can do to deprive us of our rights. If they still choose to do so, we have a remedy.

But at the heart of the reason that people rush to take legal recourse is the fact that the courts have become the last bastion of protection of the queer community from state excesses, a hostile society, a disinterested legislature and violent natal families. Often, the courts have been the best, if not the only, source of support for the community. Yet, as was evident from the tone and tenor of the judges in the marriage equality litigation, the arguments for the Union of India, and various states during the marriage equality petition, the courts have to walk a tightrope. Judicial activism has now become a dirty word, something that must not be done. In this process, the Supreme Court gives up its hitherto admirable legacy of standing up to majoritarian governments, and the executive has post-2014 won almost all major cases.[8] This is happening more and more now, as the court becomes aware of the limits of its own political capital, and has perhaps given too much leeway to the executive infringement on fundamental rights. As Indira Jaising writes:

> If the Constitution of India has any value, it is that it contains Article 226 and Article 32 which enable the courts to give binding directions to the government, which are the heart and soul of the Constitution. It is these Articles that are endangered today. The body of the judiciary has self-inflicted wounds.[9]

Traditionally, the courts in the United States and sometimes in India would stay away from questions that were political in nature. This would include matters like questions on policy, say, on foreign policy or how the government spent its money. This is called the doctrine of political thicket. However, with the public interest litigation (PIL) jurisdiction, that difference was obfuscated. The courts decided and laid down the law (often legislating) on a variety of issues from the rights of prisoners, to environmental issues, and prevention of sexual harassment and corruption. The Indian judiciary has a proud tradition of being activist and often taking on legislative and executive functions. The Supreme Court and the high courts must not shy away from this. Rather, they must embrace it.

Some litigation in the public interest is successful, like the striking down of Section 377, while some like the one seeking horizontal reservation through a clarification of the National Legal Services Authority (NALSA) are not. Some litigation like the challenge to the Transgender Persons (Protection of Right) Act, 2019, is lost in the sea of backlogs that the courts have. Efforts of activists and lawyers might be reduced to naught if the courts themselves stick to restraint and defer to majoritarianism. It is also not as if the courts do not increasingly interfere in political matters. In recent times, for example, the court has sat in judicial review and come down heavily on the actions of governors, whereby they refused to assent to bills, or sent them to the President, passed by the legislatures in Tamil Nadu and Kerala. Increasingly, political disputes are making their way to the Supreme Court, and it is hearing and adjudicating them—in some cases, it nudges; in others, it brokers peace between rivals. So for the court to stay away from answering political questions, in the sole garb of the fact that they are political is, in my view, a cop-out.

* * *

'Life of the law,' wrote Justice Oliver Wendell Holmes in his book *The Common Law*, 'has not been logic: it has been experience. The felt necessities of the time, the prevalent moral and political theories, intuitions of public policy, avowed or unconscious, and even the prejudices which judges share with their fellow men, have had a good deal more to do than the syllogism in determining the rules by which men should be governed. The law embodies the story of a nation's development through many centuries, and it cannot be dealt with as if it contained only the axioms and corollaries of a book of mathematics.'[10]

When I was approached to write this book, I had already been mulling over the idea of writing a blow-by-blow account of what happened in perhaps one of the most widely watched queer rights cases in India, perhaps even more so than *Navtej* (since it was being live-streamed), and to pen down what went through my mind as a queer lawyer with the poetic arguments of Anand Grover, or the clinical precision of Dr Abhishek Manu Singhvi, or Dr Menaka Guruswamy's passionate pleas for a 'bouquet of rights' and Saurabh Kirpal's demand for the rights that the Constitution had promised us. Notably, by breaking the norm at the bar of advocating for the client, so many passionate pleas by Kirpal, Guruswamy, Katju and others spoke of the day-to-day lived realities of these lawyers themselves. Consider the following utterances:

> *'Don't make the next generation of LGBTQ citizens go through what we have been through.'*

> *'I cannot buy SCBA [Supreme Court Bar Association] insurance for my partner, My Lord.'*

> *'First we were third-class citizens; then after decriminalization, we have been reduced to second-class citizens; now we are asking for equality.'*

It was impossible for anyone in that courtroom to not tear up at such passionate pleas from lawyers who belonged to the community. These are some phrases which struck a chord with me, and I dare say with the judges. Because all judgments, both the majority and the minority note that discrimination and dehumanization are writ large in the lives of queer people. Even Justice Bhat, who wrote the majority opinion denying equality in marriage, for example, notes that, 'The feeling of exclusion that comes with this status quo, is undoubtedly one which furthers the feeling of exclusion on a daily basis, in society for members of the queer community.'[11]

At the same time, there were the arguments of the Solicitor General, dripping with venom, calling us 'these people', which under the garb of legal arguments sought to project queer people and identities as something amorphous. 'There are seventy-two shades and varieties of these identities . . . How will your lordships regulate them?' These arguments dehumanizing and almost slanderous, and I had to stop myself from reacting multiple times. When for the first time the Solicitor General said, 'There is no stigma', referring to the lives of queer people in the post-Navtej era, I could not stop groaning. Tara Narula, a lawyer who was standing next to me, yanked at my gown and stopped me just in time before I could react in a way that would have drawn more attention and earned me the ire of the judges. In that moment, the lives that we lead, of facing bullying in educational institutions and on social media, and continued discrimination, were sought to be wiped off with one off-the-cuff statement.

As you read this book, I want to position myself in two parts—first, as a queer person whose rights were the subject matter of the dispute before the court, and second, as a lawyer representing two couples. These two parts often came into conflict with one another. At times, the lawyer won. More often, he did not. Perhaps it was a side effect of being a rookie lawyer. Senior Advocate Anand Grover, who I was briefing in this matter, had to often put up with my anxieties and outbursts, and he was ever so patient with me. He held my hand through it all—drafting the petitions, written submissions and oral arguments; and, as I write this, the anxious wait for the judgment.

I also want to use this book as a springboard to have a broader conversation: about queer people, queer lawyers, the law, queerness, the Indian queer rights movement, and an amalgamation of all of these things. As I write this, we are nearing half a decade of decriminalization after Navtej Singh Johar & Ors v. Union of India. This book is as much a celebration of queerness as it is a remembrance of decades worth of legal struggles by sex workers, transgender persons, Dalit, Bahujan and Adivasi persons, and the grassroots workers who campaigned for HIV/AIDS awareness programmes, who led the fight against Section 377 since the 1990s, and who find themselves erased in the 'picture that irons out the unruly creases of historical inexplicability and is ready to adorn the manicured walls of an aesthetically curated memory museum', as Oishik Sircar and Dipika Jain put it.[12] Perhaps another way of framing the queer movement in India is quite similar to Prof. Rohit De's framing of the universal adult franchise in his book A People's Constitution—'this process was led by some of India's most marginalized citizens rather than by elite politicians and judges.'[13]

* * *

Each case has a life of its own that begins after the judgment is out. If a social justice movement has to successfully tap into the power of the law to effectuate meaningful change, it must not stop after the judgment, but use it to advocate for more reforms on the substratum that the judgment builds. A movement must use the power of litigation, the law and the power to hold the government to account through the courts. Perhaps with a majoritarian government that attacks civil society, paints all dissent as being anti-national, and makes the process into a punishment in itself through the Unlawful Activities Prevention Act, as it did with the Bhima Koregaon Activists or the Prevention of Money Laundering Act, or the Foreign Contribution Regulatory Act, the work of building a social justice movement and collectivizing through civil society has become nearly impossible. Every success comes after failures, but it is contingent on how well the movement can rally after a failure. But building movements becomes a Herculean task not because of the government itself, but the fact that the courts do not take action seeking transparency and accountability with as much force as they would otherwise have if the present dispensation was not as populist and majoritarian as it is. Take, for example, the COVID litigation. The Supreme Court, instead of directing the government to take specific steps, evolved a process of dialogic judicial review in matters of vaccination and oxygen supply. It meant that 'the judicial forum is a site of dialogue between courts, citizens, and the government; often, the very process of the government being called upon to explain its decisions before the courts reveals important shortcomings in the decision-making process (as well as in the substantive nature of the decision itself), which can then be corrected'.[14] Increasingly, the same is happening in matters of adjudication of fundamental rights. The court seems to want to engage in a dialogue, or worse, broker a middle-path solution, in cases where the issues of rights require adjudication.

For example, during the course of the marriage equality case, the court suggested that the petitioners sit with the government and try to create a set of laws and legislative reforms to enable queer people to achieve a semblance of marriage without marrying. This raises several legal, philosophical and political issues: Should matters of fundamental rights be a site of dialogue? Or do they deserve a proper adjudication? Is a dialogue possible when the government does not come to the table with good faith? I will leave you with some food for thought on that, and come back to it at a later point in this book.

* * *

Every month there is at least one new case across the high courts that deals with queer rights, mostly of queer persons seeking protection from violence. A few are even filed in the Supreme Court. For one reason or the other, they are widely covered by the media, and often make headlines on legal portals. This is something unique to the movement for queer rights in India. As a movement, we have been devoting significant resources to advancing queer liberation by channelling a major chunk of resources towards litigation in the form of challenges to various policies and laws which restrict the right to live a full life, and to conduct lives as equal citizens of a constitutional democracy. The litigation has spanned diverse areas of law—election laws, administrative laws, constitutional law, registration of names on a passport, the desire to be parents. At the heart of each of these challenges is a simple desire—to live life with dignity, autonomy, privacy and freedom. Queer persons seek little more than the equal protection of the law, the removal of discrimination and the right to free expression. They ask for equality. Nothing more and nothing less.

At the heart of the Indian constitutional governance scheme lie the powers of the Supreme Court and the high courts to protect the fundamental rights of citizens. Article 32 of the Constitution of India empowers a citizen to directly approach the Supreme Court in case of a violation of these rights. Dr Ambedkar, while speaking about Article 32, called this 'the heart and soul of the Indian Constitution'. It is because the right to approach the Supreme Court is itself a fundamental right. An analogous power exists under Article 226 for the high courts. These powers are wide and constitutional courts have used these powers to read new rights into existing rights. Consider, for example, Article 21 of the Constitution. It simply reads, 'No person shall be deprived of his life or personal liberty except according to procedure established by law.' Yet, the courts have used their power of reading into existing right new rights, such as the right to clean drinking water, the right to privacy, the right to dignity, and even the right to die with dignity. The Indian Supreme Court is called the most powerful constitutional court for a reason. Its powers are wide, wide enough to even declare an amendment to the Constitution as being unconstitutional if it violates the basic structure of the Constitution. It is the final arbiter of disputes. The power of the Court, if used wisely by both judges and lawyers to advance rights, can go a long way in honing a vision of the Constitution in light of its spirit and ideals.

So when activists and lawyers use the courts and the Constitution as a means to move closer to queer liberation, we must remember that rights cannot last if we do not tap into the power of civil society and social change. We must engage with the legal system, for we as queer people are either used as woke brownie points in a diversity section at best, and at worst as mere annexures or afterthoughts in policies. However, when we use the courts, we must challenge the legal system in itself and the way it perpetuates inequality. We must use the thrust of the social causes that we seek to champion as activists to turn the legal system into an instrument of social justice. If we do not do that, the rights that we seek to protect themselves become fallible. Eternal vigilance is the price we pay for liberty.[15]

* * *

But let me go back to the personal. A few weeks before the petitions were listed, I had my convocation ceremony from

Gujarat National Law University (GNLU). As a mark of queer solidarity, and also to make sure I went back to the campus where I hid my queerness out of shame, I decided to wear a pride stole. My photograph appeared in the press without my consent. Whether it came from the university or an enthusiastic reporter, I do not know. But I have no regrets, and indeed I am glad that the photograph made its way to the newspaper.[16]

At GNLU, I have been on the receiving end of homophobia, professors who have said homophobic things in class including stuff like 'This is a mental health problem' and 'Ab toh Supreme Court *ne kaha hai jisko jo karna hai woh karo*' (Now the Supreme Court has said anyone can do whatever they like) when I was a student in the immediate aftermath of the Navtej Singh Johar judgment. Queer students who currently study at GNLU tell me that such utterances are still made in class and even outside. A few of them have even gone public with the revelations. I did object to what was a brazen attempt to pink-wash the image of the university. However, I did not go public with my objections because the pride scarf was intended to send out a message that those of us on campus who are queer deserve a safe learning environment, which I did not receive. The symbolic value of the gesture notwithstanding, it was also meant to assert my identity in front of the world at large in a place where I had received homophobic treatment.

So when I talk about the movement and what happens in court, it is informed by lived experiences of discrimination, of being stared at when I ask for HIV tests, of landlords asking acquaintances why I spoke the way I did in front of me. These are not merely legal arguments. Nor are these arguments that I see as simply legal propositions. Family law is hardly governed by the Civil Procedure Code or the daily mundanities of the law. There are emotions, there are feelings, and there are lives of people at stake. In this case, it was lives which have been historically disenfranchised, and whose very existence was criminal until 2018. In each case, the rationality and rationalistic bargains as seen in commercial cases are lost. Especially when my own rights were being litigated, the fate of my own life and that of the community weighed on me. At every party, dinner or meeting with a friend, the conversation would invariably turn to marriage equality. Causal ties to rationality become tenuous then. The subject of the law then is not a benefit-toting or power-driven individual or a corporation with commercial interest, it is me: I am no longer just a lawyer on the case, I am also a subject of litigation without being a petitioner. One then starts to see the law not as the Austinian adage of being 'command of sovereign backed by sanction', but as the dictator of heart, mind, emotions and psyche. Such cases are not a dispute of not following the law but a situation where one is unwillingly the subject of the law, seeking to establish a hearth, to associate not in the expressive but the intimate sense, to want domesticity and to move away from the political passions of the law and emotionless constitutional reason into one driven by passion and intimacy.

Before writing this chapter, I was reading through my own writings on marriage equality, and I came to realize that my own perspective on law has changed. A piece that I wrote in the *Indian Express*[17] which rebutted arguments by Tahir Mahmood[18] was how I usually thought about the law, and how I have been trained to think clinically about it. It is a fixed procedure. Frame your arguments, listen to the opponent's arguments, and respond to them. But as we got closer in time to the case, much emotion flooded into my writing. After a particularly homophobic piece by Prof. G.S. Bajpai et al,[19] I wrote in *The Hindu*:

> This is not to argue that marriage will lead to queer liberation. In fact, marriage does not obfuscate but lays bare the caste hierarchies that embolden discrimination and segregation. But despite being a faulty institution, marriage is a legitimate legal need in order to file taxes jointly, inherit property, open bank accounts, and choose nominees for insurance policies . . . Queer people cannot wait until society thinks it is acceptable for us to have rights. We refuse to be polite citizens, we will continue to be unapologetic about our sexuality, and we will continue to challenge widespread notions of respectability, of marriage, and procreation. We refuse to cower in the terror of knowing that the only way we can survive is if we are smart, lucky, or are fighters. We demand that notions of family and traditions be broadened and notions of acceptability and respectability be demolished. Legal recognition of queerness and love should not be opposed by the state or by some supposedly well-meaning proponents of the doctrine of separation of powers. Queerness and queer love deserve not just legal recognition by the state, but to be celebrated.[20]

I realize, as I read the piece now, that I was no longer thinking, as I usually did of law—rationally and devoid of emotions. Blood rushed through my veins in anger when I saw homophobia masquerading as a legal argument, and there was a joy which can best be described as queer euphoria when I was working on this case. Should I have, as a lawyer, gotten personally invested in the case? Conventional wisdom would dictate otherwise. Yet, it was hard not to.

Let me end with a caveat. One can be emotional, yet one cannot be irrational. As Solomon said, it is good 'to know wisdom and instruction; to perceive the words of understanding; to receive the instruction of wisdom, justice, and judgement, and equity; to give subtlety to the simple, to the young man knowledge and discretion'.[21] It is to say, that when injustice is manifest in the law, justice should not be blind to empathy. An empathetic reading of the law was required in the case. We must remember that our constitutional courts are not merely courts of law, but also courts of equity. But I would go further and argue, they should also be courts of justice. The courts are, in our legal system, the last institution where a citizen can get redress from state excesses. It is thus, imperative, that they deliver justice and do that with empathy.

The truth will eventually out. I am writing this exactly one month before Justice Ravindra Bhat, who was on the bench, retires. We should have the judgment in the next month. My nights are growing sleepless; I have had nightmares of being cross-examined by the judges on the bench as if I were an accused, and some even about a Koushal-like moment where the judgment goes against the queer community and the court holds that there is no requirement for the right to marry a person of one's choice if one is queer. Though the minuscule minority jurisprudence of Koushal is long gone, its ghosts continue to haunt the queer community and me.

Let me answer one question I often get asked about this case. Did we have an open-and-shut case? The answer to that was perhaps no, in retrospect. I did believe that we had a slam dunk in our favour at the beginning. Yet, there were curveballs which I did not anticipate at the beginning of the case. But I will not spill the beans. Read on and find out.

Chapter 2

A Judicial Punch in the Gut
and the Way Forward

*The Queens are poor and raunchy. They live on what others no longer
want. They have no power. They have no social place. They almost
have no allies. All this makes them angry and amused. It makes
then restless and out of place. It makes them high-spirited
and disruptive. They know it takes all kinds to make the revolutions.
Others do now know this yet. The Queens are out and are not
coming back. They wait for the others to join them.*
—Larry Mitchell, *The Faggots and Their
Friends between Revolutions*[1]

It had been a difficult few months for queer people around
the country. The Supreme Court had concluded ten days of
complex legal arguments in Supriyo Chakraborty v. Union of
India and scores of other cases which were tagged and heard
together a few months ago. Queer people, allies and even
opponents across the country had been glued to their screens for
the ten days of those arguments. Complex legalese like 'indirect
discrimination', 'workability model' and 'constitutional
comity', which perhaps have no meaning to people who are
not lawyers, were being thrown around in court. That is what

keeps us lawyers employed: Sesquipedalian words, beyond the comprehension of mere mortals who do not have the letters LLB after their names. The sparring between lawyers and judges was being reported (and misreported) widely in both social and traditional media during the hearings, and the country waited with bated breath. The argument had seen interventions from a lot of uninvited guests who had little, if anything, to do with the issue. I guess when there is a wedding, gatecrashers and unwelcome guests must be expected. The day would finally dawn—as the retirement of Justice Bhat drew near, one could feel the community growing palpably more restless with every passing day. But we could do little more than wait.

* * *

On the evening of 16 October 2023, I was returning to Delhi with Mr Anand Grover, a senior advocate that I work with along with Ms Indira Jaising, after having just argued a case in the Bombay High Court, when my phone suddenly became uncharacteristically abuzz. I was getting multiple messages from friends, family, a few friends in the media and even a few unknown numbers. 'Is it true??', 'Are the reports confirmed?', 'What is happening???' I had no clue. It turned out that Bar and Bench, one of India's two major legal online portals, had just broken the story that the verdict in the marriage equality case was supposed to be delivered the next morning. My heart was in my mouth. I went to the Supreme Court website. The supplementary cause list, which is the list of cases which the court will hear or pronounce judgments on in a given day, in addition to the main cause list, was not out yet.

Where was this information coming from? I called up friends who worked with Live Law and Bar and Bench and asked them if it was true. They confirmed that sources from within the Supreme Court had told them that the judgment would be delivered the next day. Strange that the news outlets had the news before it was officially declared. This has now happened multiple times since then, and it does not bode well for the court's institutional integrity if media outlets know through 'sources' about what is happening inside the court. At the same time, my heart was in my mouth. At the airport, Mr Grover perhaps saw how anxious I was and offered to buy me a drink. I refused, for I was not sure that I could keep anything down. The marriage equality case was the third case in which I had got to assist a senior before a Constitution bench. But I had never been as nervous as I was for this case. As we boarded the flight, I took my SOS anxiety medication to avoid the panic attack I knew was inevitable, and slept.

As soon as we landed, I checked the website again. The cause list was out. And lo and behold, there was the following notice:

SUPREME COURT OF INDIA
[IT WILL BE APPRECIATED IF THE LEARNED ADVOCATES ON RECORD DO NOT SEEK ADJOURNMENT IN THE MATTERS LISTED BEFORE ALL THE COURTS IN THE CAUSE LIST]
DAILY CAUSE LIST FOR DATED : 17-10-2023
CHIEF JUSTICE'S COURT
HON'BLE THE CHIEF JUSTICE
HON'BLE MR. JUSTICE SANJAY KISHAN KAUL
HON'BLE MR. JUSTICE S. RAVINDRA BHAT
HON'BLE MS. JUSTICE HIMA KOHLI
HON'BLE MR. JUSTICE PAMIDIGHANTAM SRI NARASIMHA
(TIME : 10:30 AM)

NOTE :
Whenever written submissions are directed to be filed by the Court in any proceeding, advocates and parties in person are requested to email a soft copy in a pdf form on or before the stipulated date to the following email id :

cmvc.dyc@gmail.com

The soft copies which are emailed should not be scanned copies of printed submissions. No other documents other than written submissions should be filed in this email.

NOTE:-
[SPECIAL BENCH]
SUPPLEMENTARY LIST

SNo.	Case No.	Petitioner / Respondent	Petitioner/Respondent Advocate

FOR JUDGEMENT

1501	W.P.(C) No. 1011/2022 PIL-W	SUPRIYO @ SUPRIYA CHAKRABORTY AND ANR.	PRIYA PURI
		Versus UNION OF INDIA	
			VIKASH CHANDRA SHUKLA [INT], SWATI GHILDIYAL [INT], SWARUPAMA CHATURVEDI[INT], SURYA KANT[INT], SURBHI KAPOOR [INT], SUNNY CHOUDHARY[INT]

It was confirmed. The judgment would be delivered the next day. My phone was already buzzing with calls from journalists in India, the UK, the US and other countries around the world. They wanted to know what would happen tomorrow, if I knew which way the judgment would go, and what it would mean for the queer community. I told them all the same thing: We would know the answers to all of these questions at 10.30 a.m. the next day. Until the judgment was out, it was impossible to answer those questions. A news outlet wanted a quote from me before the judgment the next morning on the Supreme Court lawns. I did say yes, but I knew I would not be in the right state of mind to do so.

That night was the toughest night of my life. I tossed and turned in my bed and couldn't sleep all night. I went back to the petitions, to the written submissions looking for things that could have gone wrong or arguments against us. What could we have done differently was the question I kept on asking myself. Perhaps, I knew subconsciously that the judgment would not go in our favour.

The next morning, I woke up, took a quick shower and was ready to go. I am hardly superstitious, but that day I felt I had to be. I wore everything I thought would help: A pride lapel pin, cufflinks given to me by a lover and the first pair of lawyer's bands I ever bought. A bit of good juju never hurt anyone.

The courtroom was bustling with chatter and was jam-packed. We reached at about 10.20 a.m. and had to fight our way to the front. In the crowd of people inside the court of the Chief Justice, I noticed friends, petitioners, lawyers and others. The tension in the room was palpable. It was electrifying. You could hear nervous laughter, tears, chuckles, sobs, guffaws, and whispers about the latest gossip on which way the judgment was going. 10.30, 10.35, 10.45—the judges were still not there. A look at the display board told us that none of the benches of the court had assembled. 'Justice Bhat is retiring, and they are clicking pictures. The Chief is leaving tomorrow,' said a voice. One did not know what to believe.

It was not to be so for long, yet it felt like decades. At about 10.55 a.m., the judges entered the courtroom and folded their hands in a namaste; we bowed. There is an English tradition that we follow at the Indian bar, which I think holds great importance. When the judges enter the courtroom, they bow to the lawyers, or some fold their hands in namaste, and the lawyers reciprocate. This tradition is traced back to when the first Royal Coat of Arms was created in 1399 during the reign of King Henry IV. They appeared then inside every courtroom in England and Wales. It was a symbol that justice comes from the monarch, and that a law court is part of the Royal Court. When solicitors and barristers bowed in England, they bowed to the coat of arms, and not the judge. This has now become a sign of the mutual respect that the bar and the bench have for each other.

As soon as they sat, the Chief Justice proclaimed, 'There is a level of agreement, and a level of disagreement. We have only disagreed with how far we can go.' You could see the smiles in the courtroom on the side of the petitioners. I am sure I even saw some tears. I teared up too, confident of the win, at least a partial one. I thought that if nothing, they would have given us the right to marry, and that we would live to fight another day. Alas, it was not to be.

* * *

The pronouncement of the judgment went on for over three hours. By some accounts, it was the longest pronouncement in open court of a judgement that had been reserved. I do not know if it is true, but it did feel so. Each minute, the noose around our neck felt tighter. Each second was more dreadful than the previous. Hope seemed lost. Each new sentence was a punch in the gut. Unanimously, all five judges of the court had held that there was no fundamental right to marry for queer persons. That was when we knew that not only was this a disastrous loss for the queer rights movement, but also for the fundamental rights jurisprudence in the country. It confirmed what a lot of us had been saying for a while, in public and in private: The court was collapsing against executive pressure, and that it was in a recession of protecting civil liberties. In the past few months, as I write this, the Supreme Court has not interfered with the alacrity that was demanded in what is called 'bulldozer justice', where houses of mostly Muslims were demolished without due process, for example. But the Supreme Court has always been a 'fair-weather' friend to the fundamental rights jurisprudence: When there is significant resistance to judicial interference and activism from majoritarian governments, it has acquiesced. This is not merely a post-2014 phenomenon. Even during the Emergency imposed by Mrs Indira Gandhi, the Supreme Court, in Additional District Magistrate, Jabalpur v. Shivkant Shukla,[2] held that the right to life and liberty can be suspended during Emergency. At the same time, when the government is weak, the court has pushed back and expanded fundamental rights jurisprudence. However, the court has, since 2014, forgotten that it is supposed to serve as a counter-majoritarian force against executive excesses. It has now become a site for dialogue between the oppressor-majoritarian state and the oppressed, instead of being a site for adjudication.

Of course, there is a larger question which needs to be addressed on whether the courts are an appropriate forum to further the cause of social justice movements. There have been debates about whether litigation is an appropriate tool to drive policy in the United States, India and other countries. However, with the advent of the public interest litigation in India, courts have virtually legislated on issues like sexual harassment, prison conditions and police atrocities. So, even assuming that we were telling the court to legislate (which we were not), there was no reason for the court to not do it, except for the fact that it was dealing with vehement pushback on social media, from fringe groups, by Bharatiya Janata Party (BJP) parliamentarians like Sushil Modi, the then law minister Kiren Rijiju and even the Bar Council of India.[3] And buckle the court did. Before we go into the critique of the judgment as well as the arguments in the book, let us look at what it broadly summed up:

1. There were four judgments which were delivered by the court: Justices Ravindra Bhat and Hima Kohli wrote the majority opinion, Justice P.S. Narsimha concurred with them but wrote a separate opinion, and Justices D.Y. Chandrachud and Sanjay Kishan Kaul wrote separate dissenting opinions.

2. All five judges unanimously held that the right to marry is not a fundamental right, ignoring their own previous judgments. They further held that consequently, any state action or legislation which leads to deprivation of the right to marry is not violative of Articles 14, 19(1)(a) and 21 of the Indian Constitution.

3. Save for Justice Sanjay Kishan Kaul, all other judges held that the Special Marriage Act (SMA) was

constitutionally valid. Justice Kaul struck it down, holding that the SMA was an example of a larger and deeper form of structural discrimination against queer people, which was constitutionally impermissible.

4. There was a 3:2 split (Justices Bhat, Narasimha and Kohli speaking for the majority) on the issue of adoption. The majority held that Section 57(2) of the Juvenile Justice Act, 2015, which provided for adoption rights to 'couple[s]', could be construed to be extending only to married couples. As a logical sequitur, queer people did not have a right to adopt since they could not marry.

5. On the issue of Regulation 5(3) of the Adoption Regulations, 2022, which provided for adoption for people with 'two years of stable marital relationship', was also constitutionally permissible, and further deprived queer people from adopting.

6. Yet, the bench held that the effective prohibition on queer couples jointly adopting a child is indirectly discriminatory. With a 3:2 split (Justices Bhat, Narasimha and Kohli speaking for the majority), the court held that such indirect discrimination can only be 'suitably redressed and removed by the State', and the Supreme Court cannot fashion any remedy for queer people.

7. Finally, with a 3:2 split (Justices Bhat, Narasimha and Kohli again speaking for the majority), the court held that a combined reading of Articles 19(1)(c), 19(1)(e), 21 and 25 did not merit the imposition of a 'positive obligation' on the Union to recognize any relationship such as a 'civil union' of same-sex couples;

8. The court also held unanimously, that transgender persons in heterosexual relationships can marry both under religious personal law and the Special Marriage Act.

The reading of the judgment went on for the entirety of the morning session of the court, what I am told was the longest reading in public memory. Afterwards, everyone left the court hurt, dejected and upset. A few people were nonchalant. Some of us could not believe this had happened. My phone was buzzing again with requests from the media. I could not answer. I had an anxiety attack and had to compose myself before I could be presentable before a camera or form coherent sentences.

I was heavily bullied as a kid. For the way I looked, the way I spoke, the way I walked. This is not uncommon for queer kids. Some of us, like Arvey, who died by suicide after being horribly abused by his classmates, and Pranshu, who took his own life after being trolled mercilessly for his make-up videos, pay for this treatment with our lives.[4] In my case, the bullying gave rise to some deep-seated insecurities which persist to this day, and as a result, I prefer not to speak to the media on television. I have always believed that my role as a lawyer is to argue cases in court and not in a television debate. That, of course, is not to deride those lawyers who do go on television (for it is a common thing to do at the bar), for I believe that they perform important tasks of public education, shaping public debates and opinions and raising awareness. But I choose, as far as I can, not to be on television unless I think the issue is such that it requires a nuance which other lawyers may not be able to bring out and I can on account of my lived experiences.

But it dawned on me that now was not the time to think of myself and my insecurities. It was time to give a call to action to the nation and the queer community. I went out and gave a few sound bites and spoke my mind about the judgment. I still remember, while I was speaking to NDTV, I told the interviewer that this was a 'judicial punch in the gut of the queer movement', and 'that we will rise, rage, love harder, and come out stronger'. This was pure rage coming out, and I think it took everything in my power to not say things that would amount to contempt of court, and to continue to be reverential.

As I went out of the court premises and back to the office, my mind kept on going back to words from Larry Mitchell's book *The Faggots and Their Friends between Revolutions*. It goes something like this:

> The strong women told the faggots that there are two important things to remember about the coming revolutions. The first is that we will get our asses kicked. The second is that we will win. The faggots knew the first. Faggot ass-kicking is a time-honored sport of the men. But the faggots did not know about the second. They had never thought about winning before. They did not even know what winning meant. So they asked the strong women and the strong women said winning was like surviving, only better. As the strong women explained winning, the faggots were surprised and then excited. The faggots knew about surviving for they always had and this was going to be just plain better. That made ass-kicking different. Getting your ass kicked and then winning elevated the entire enterprise of making revolution.[5]

This is one of my favourite passages, but that day, after getting my ass kicked, it did not feel like I would ever win. My faith in the Constitution and its abilities to ensure justice was shaken and scarred and gouged and stripped and bombed.

This was not the first time that the queer movement had lost in the courts, but this was the first time that I had been a part of that loss, and my own criminality and culpability in it seemed unforgivable. There was obvious blowback from within the queer community on these petitions after the loss and even prior to it, mainly on the fact that there was no wider community consultation before filing the petitions, or not enough advocacy and awareness. Perhaps it was unwise to have rushed to the Supreme Court when matters were pending before the high courts. But what was done was done. There was no point in assigning blame. The next steps had to be twofold: First, processing our queer grief, and second, figuring out how to fight back.

But how do we anatomize social movement litigation for us to be able to effectively navigate its turbulent waters? When we seek the coercive power of a judicial pronouncement without building a social movement and we lose, how do we get up? How do we deal with a complex charter of demands that arise from multiple petitions spanning over what the judges called a 'spider's web' of legislations, which often clash with each other, or, if they don't, are still diverse yet similar enough to be heard together? How do we reconcile these demands?

The legal canon of a social justice lawyer is what led me to want to go to law school since I was seven. Atticus Finch. Gloria Allred. Nani Palkhivala. Fali Nariman. Ambedkar. These were the lawyers I wanted to be like. I knew, as a fifteen-year-old, that I wanted to be talking about the Constitution in the courts, and outside of it, after reading *Freedom at Midnight* by Larry Collins and Dominique Lapierre. And the fact that I get to do this, that I have been able to assist seniors in multiple Constitution bench litigations, is a dream come true. I do this because I believe in how the legal historian Kenneth Mack framed the purpose of the law. In the context of the United States Constitution, he wrote:

> [C]ourts as the primary engines of social transformation; formal conceptual categories such as rights and formal remedies such as school desegregation decrees as the principal mechanisms for accomplishing that change; and . . . reforming public institutions (or, in some versions, public and private institutions without much distinction) as a means of transforming the larger society.[6]

I think, with the power of our Constitution and its transformative character, and with the willingness of judges of the constitutional courts, social justice lawyers can play a much wider role, not just in effectuating change in society, but also in the courts and the legal profession. I have seen my own senior, Indira Jaising, do it in multiple cases. But one case in her career which stands out for me is the senior designation case.

The Indian legal profession consists of two kinds of advocates: Senior advocates and advocates. Senior advocates are 'designated' by the Supreme Court or the high court; they wear a silk robe, a *monkey* (yes, you read it right) jacket and charge magnificent fees. They do so on account of their knowledge or standing at the bar.[7] To be designated, one requires a full court resolution which is voted on by the judges to that effect. For the first time, in 2015, Jaising challenged the process on the grounds that it had become arbitrary and only those with the right connections could be designated. She asked for the following prayers:

(a) Issue writ, order, or direction declaring that the system of designation of Senior Advocates by recently introduced method of vote is arbitrary and contrary to the notions of diversity violating Articles 14, 15 and 21 and therefore, it is unconstitutional and null and void; and

.

.

.

(c) Issue a writ of mandamus or direction directing Respondent 1 representing the Chief Justice and the Judges of the Supreme Court to appoint a Search Committee to identify the Advocates who conduct public interest litigation (PIL) cases and Advocates who practice in the area of their domain expertise viz. constitutional law, international arbitration, inter-State water disputes, cyber laws, etc. and to designate them as Senior Advocates.[8]

She succeeded in her endeavour then, and the Supreme Court laid down detailed guidelines on making the process of designation more transparent. Subsequently, the matter came up for hearing again sometime in 2023 on a modification application filed. This time, I had the chance to assist her with the case. Such was the force of her arguments, in court, as also in her written submissions, that she succeeded in making sure that diversity, and being a first-generation lawyer, was given due credit in designating senior advocates. In something that was unheard of, in 2024, the Supreme Court for the first time designated eleven women lawyers, and thirty-four first-generation lawyers as senior advocates in a historic first. This included Shobha Gupta, who was the lawyer for Bilkis Bano.[9] Most senior advocates are men, usually upper-caste and upper-class, whose families have been in the legal profession for generations. In a profession that is not resistant but perhaps immune to change, I have seen Jaising break glass ceilings and use the power of the Constitution and law to force its hand to change. This was also why I chose to work with her. In her eighties, she is still a force of nature.

At the same time, I am of course, not blind to the criticisms of critical legal scholars who have argued that there are limitations on the capacity of the courts to bring about social change.[10] Change, if any, must come from society. They also argue that victories in court cases give only small, pyrrhic victories.[11] This call came from the inside of the queer movement, and also from fierce trans rights activists who I have admired both during the decriminalization litigation as well as the marriage equality litigation. A. Revathi, a trans rights activist, in the backdrop of the Navtej Singh Johar judgment, said, 'We're still being policed on our food, dress, consumption, writing [and] choices, by the society, government and its machinery . . . Murders, rapes, thefts, false charges, shootouts and lots of other problems will not allow us to celebrate the [Section] 377 [strike-down] tomorrow. We all know who is going to benefit out of this.'[12] These criticisms were made also after the marriage equality litigation.

Similarly, a lot of voices during the marriage equality litigation also opposed it for not being inclusive, for not building consensus, and for being 'Delhi-centric'. These are not charges that I can deny, but those that I plead guilty to. I only wish to provide my defence.

There are other pressing issues which are on hand, such as the ban on the Transgender Persons (Protection of Rights) Act, the ban on conversion therapy and horizontal reservations for transgender persons, amongst others. For me, the marriage equality litigation was not so much about marriage as it was for asserting the right to equality and queerness in the courts.

But for some reason, this case jumped the docket for reasons best known to the powers that be.

We are at a phase in the queer movement where we have seen that it is increasingly becoming lawyer-centric. For the smallest of issues, people seem to rush to the Supreme Court. What this frequently results in is half-baked petitions, and often damage to the movement itself. While in any legal discourse on rights in India, the Constitution is a sine qua non, using it as the only weapon that a movement can wield does not serve the purpose. It must be a major tool in the toolbox but be complemented with other tools such as social realities and historical facts so that the complexities of the lives led by the people of this country are accurately captured in petitions. We have not done that so far, save for a few instances. I do not blame the clients who often do not know the right course of action. I blame the lawyers who take certain matters to court. They must guide their clients appropriately. But they do not, for the wide reportage of queer issues has turned litigating such issues, often without a basic understanding of the community itself, into a cake that everyone wants a piece of, often with self-serving interests. 'I want to do LGBT cases and become famous,' (sic) an unsuspecting lawyer once told me. This of course also results in the movement being co-opted by lawyers, as we have been warned against repeatedly.

We can, however, avoid this. As I was saying, there is now a new age of social movements and social justice litigation which is informed by a State which is increasingly clamping down on civil society in the form of tax raids, choking funding, jailing dissidents under terror laws, criminalizing any form of dissent, making free speech nearly impossible. When issues like marriage equality are taken up in the Supreme Court, which affects the rights of the queer community at large, the time has come for a more participative process to evolve in the system. Unlike other movements, like the feminist movements, where on broad issues there is a seeming consensus, the queer movement lacks one. That is primarily because there are not enough places where conversations can take place, or platforms where the community can discuss issues, irrespective of our disagreements, howsoever vehement they may be. Yet, when PILs are filed in the Supreme Court, they do affect the community at large. As a result, what we have is that many members of the community who may not be in Delhi or urban India are left out of conversations and eventually disenfranchised. This becomes more acute when much of the movement is judicialized. I do not dispute that in cases where the rights of an individual are violated, they should be free to move the court. However, when issues like marriage equality are filed as PILs, it calls for a participative litigation that is more inclusive and collaborative. When I talk about a collaborative litigation strategy, I do not mean merely on which issues to take to court and when, but the broader set of decisions, including negotiating legal strategy, sounding out arguments, etc. If we, as lawyers who represent queer causes and are also queer, think of ourselves as leaders or are projected by the media to be leaders of the movement (and we usually do, because of our own hubris), we must acknowledge that there is a multiplicity of political voices within the community. All of them must be heard, and a litigation strategy must be decided in a consultative process. We cannot create a movement and centre it on a radical critique of existing power hierarchies if they manifest within our movements too. When we have created a movement around litigation—and I admit to my part in it—I also believe that we as lawyers should be held to account by the movement.

There has to be an accountability mechanism, which focuses on centring the movement's participation in the litigation process. We cannot be hostile to grassroots activists, or to the tireless work of community organizers, but see them as equal participants, where they are not dismissed to make the most perfunctory decisions in legal strategies if they are involved, or worse, as a means to an end by providing lawyers with petitioners.

In litigation-driven movements like the queer rights movement, lawyers have to remember that there are competing interests of the petitioners, often on the same side of the debate. For example, in the marriage equality case, Rituparna Borah's petition went on a different tangent, seeking recognition of chosen families on account of violence from natal family, and was not per se a petition seeking marriage. The process of drafting and arguing these petitions, therefore, must be democratic, and transcend the bounds of the traditional lawyer–client relationship. In a typical scenario, a client comes to the lawyer with the facts of the case and relies on his expertise as a legal professional to supply the requisite legal advice and guide the client on possible outcomes. However, in public interest cases, the client often arrives with the outcomes that they want to be reached, and the lawyer has to mould the law and the legal arguments to arrive at it and reverse engineer the case. Clients in these cases often know more about the issue than the lawyers themselves (and dare I say, that includes the law), and it is imperative that we tap into their lived experiences and knowledge as important resources.

The second reason I say that this process must be participatory is because litigation has become the last bastion of democracy in India, which is in peril. It is a tool that is used not just for creating policy, where the courts have engaged in a dialogue with the executive to create policy (such as the creation of a Draft National Policy on Supply and Disposal of Sanitary Napkins in Schools which arose out of a PIL[13]). In these cases, a court often nudges the executive to create a policy, though the coercive power of a judicial direction hangs on the executive's head like the sword of Damocles. In a second scenario, the PIL jurisdiction of the Supreme Court is also used to plug holes in the implementation of an already existing policy, such as the litigation around stubble burning. In both of these cases, the Supreme Court has undoubtedly played the role of the policymaker and the executor of the policy (albeit through coercing the executive to do it), defying the traditional separation of power doctrine. Litigation, in this model, becomes a tool of checks and balances against the excess or inaction of the State.

The third reason for why litigation of this nature must be participative, is because the interests of the community are at stake, and the community thus becomes an epistemic subject. The creation of new legal paradigms through litigation is arguably the creation of new knowledge building up on two things: The factum of the lived experiences of the PIL petitioners and the evolution and reformation of the existing legal norms. There is thus not just an intellectual dimension to such a litigation strategy which allows us to tap into the community and its lived experiences to further constitutional goals through multidisciplinary legal actions, but also an ethical dimension which seeks to create incremental reform and undo past injustices. If as lawyers we continue to manifest and recreate exclusionary power structures, without focusing on reform, empowerment and restoration, this battle will be lost before it has even begun.

The fourth reason for creating a participative movement is that we need to foster and nurture a culture of intersectionality, where we build solidarities not just with other movements but also within the movement. I say this for two reasons—the first is the normative good that intersectionality provides. But if that does not sit well with people—for some right-wing queer activists have accused others of 'shoving intersectionality down [their] throats'[14] or calling it a 'malaise'[15]—then I suggest they do it for a selfish reason, that the movements are working towards common goals. To understand this, I go back to the original idea that Kimberlé Crenshaw demonstrated on how the discourse of violence against women left out women of colour.[16] Similarly, within the broader queer rights movement, and in my conversation with activists across the country and ideologies, there seems to be a point where the cis queer rights movement is divorcing itself from the trans rights movement. There is a distrust for cis groups within trans groups, and rightfully so, that cis activists have demonstrated recalcitrance in their activism at best, and opposed issues surrounding trans rights issues such as challenges to the Transgender Persons (Protection of Rights) Act, 2019, or the movement for horizontal reservations at worst. As Dhiren Borsia writes:

Two days before the Delhi pride, a protest was called at the same place where the pride was supposed to culminate. Only thirty people showed up to this protest, against the 7000 that walked in the pride. Where are our priorities? Where is the queer movement? Is the celebration of this verdict just a celebration of a moment and not a movement? Because for sure it has erased the contributions of trans* people and sex workers and the women's movement and the anti-caste movement to make this moment even imaginable. When the LGBTQ+ pride can conveniently choose to ignore the T that is a part of its acronym, I dare say, I have very little faith that it would remember the Dalits, Bahujans, Adivasis, and Muslims that make a majority in all of these categories.[17]

My conversations with activists, members from the community, and even lawyers litigating queer issues across the country tell me that this distrust has only grown after the marriage equality litigation and the case jumping the docket while petitions challenging the Transgender Persons (Protection of Rights) Act filed years ago have not yet been taken up. The law in this way has become a site for marginalization itself. Creating a participative litigation movement will go a long way in addressing this distrust. The second proposal, as I said, is building inter-movement solidarity. Take for example the movement for horizontal reservations for transgender persons. The queer community must build bonds with the anti-caste movement which advocates for reservations within it.

In a final blow to the old canon and paradigmatic lawyering, the time has come now to evolve social justice litigation into a wider movement and pay attention to the courts as well as to the intersections of law and policy. No longer can we afford to be blind to the politics and how it affects the courts. Take for instance the judgment in *Supriyo*. This judgment is symptomatic of the recent functioning of the Supreme Court, in what Manu Sebastian calls 'illegal but permissible' jurisprudence.[18]

Look at some examples, including those that Manu himself cites. The way Babri Masjid was demolished was illegal, but let the Muslims have 5 acres of land elsewhere and build a temple where the masjid stood, the court said. The floor test in Maharashtra was illegal, held the court, and declined to grant any relief since the chief minister had resigned prior to the floor test. The Enforcement Directorate director was appointed illegally but the court decided to let him continue because it was supposedly in the national interest. The marriage equality judgment is yet another example where the Supreme Court notes, almost unanimously, that there is indirect discrimination but finds it permissible to allow it to happen citing supposed institutional limitations. The majority looks at minutiae by examining how recognition of marriages is discrimination but holds that there is no 'right' to any entitlement from any kind of union, official or unofficial, and ignores the massive constitutional question of discrimination staring them in the face. It is becoming evident that the Supreme Court is shying away from upsetting the executive post-2014 save for two major cases, the National Judicial Appointments Commission (NJAC) case[19] and the electoral bonds[20] case, but yet trying unsuccessfully to stand up for the fundamental rights of citizens. See, for example, the directions that the Chief Justice lays down in his 277-page minority opinion which forms the bulk of the marriage equality judgment. He directs the Union and the state governments to:

i. Ensure that the queer community is not discriminated against because of their gender identity or sexual orientation;

ii. Ensure that there is no discrimination in access to goods and services to the queer community, which are available to the public;

iii. Take steps to sensitizse the public about queer identity, including that it is natural and not a mental disorder;

iv. Establish hotline numbers that the queer community can contact when they face harassment and violence in any form;

v. Establish and publicize the availability of 'safe houses' or Garima Grehs in all districts to provide shelter to members of the queer community who are facing violence or discrimination;

vi. Ensure that 'treatments' offered by doctors or other persons, which aim to change gender identity or sexual orientation are ceased with immediate effect;

vii. Ensure that intersex children are not forced to undergo operations with regard only to their sex, especially at an age at which they are unable to fully comprehend and consent to such operations;

viii. Recognize the self-identified gender of all persons, including transgender persons, hijras and others with sociocultural identities in India, as male, female or third gender. No person shall be forced to undergo hormonal therapy or sterilization or any other medical procedure either as a condition or prerequisite to grant legal recognition to their gender identity or otherwise;

ix. The appropriate government under the Mental Healthcare Act must formulate modules covering the mental health of queer persons in their programmes under Section 29(1). Programmes to reduce suicides and attempted suicides (envisaged by Section 29[2]) must include provisions which tackle queer identity;

He further directs the police to ensure the following:

i. There shall be no harassment of queer couples by summoning them to the police station or visiting their places of residence solely to interrogate them about their gender identity or sexual orientation;

ii. They shall not force queer persons to return to their natal families if they do not wish to return to them;

iii. When a police complaint is filed by queer persons alleging that their family is restraining their freedom of movement, they shall on verifying the genuineness of the complaint ensure that their freedom is not curtailed;

iv. When a police complaint is filed apprehending violence from the family for the reason that the complainant is queer or is in a queer relationship, they shall on verifying the genuineness of the complaint ensure due protection; and

v. Before registering an FIR against a queer couple or one of the parties in a queer relationship (where the FIR is sought to be registered in relation to their relationship), they shall conduct a preliminary investigation in terms of Lalita Kumari v. Government of UP to ensure that the complaint discloses a cognizable offence. The police must first determine if the person is an adult. If the person is an adult and is in a consensual relationship with another person of the same or different gender or has left their natal home of their own volition, the police shall close the complaint after recording a statement to that effect.

All of this is fair and good. Yet, none of this was new. However, the majority does not even think it fit to give these rights to queer couples. Justice Bhat writes, 'Framework containing obligations would cast responsibilities upon private citizens and not merely the State. The learned Chief Justice's conclusions also do not point towards directions of the kind contemplated in Vishaka (supra).' This reasoning is dubious at best. Nor do the directions which the Chief Justice lay down become binding, since this is in a minority judgment. Yet, as Justice Douglas wrote in the 1960s:

> It is the right of dissent, not the right or duty to conform, which gives dignity, worth, and individuality to man. The right to dissent is the only thing that makes life tolerable for a judge of an appellate court . . . the affairs of government could not be conducted by democratic standards without it.[21]

Imagine you are an artist who is commissioned to paint a portrait. Every time you make a brush stroke, however, the canvas grows smaller. The person who commissioned you first tells you that they do not want the face to be painted. A few days later, they tell you that the arms and the legs are not to be painted. Yet, when the painting is ready, the person complains that it only has the torso. It sounds absurd. Yet, this is exactly what happened in the marriage equality case. In the first instance, we were told that the bench would only hear challenges to the SMA and leave out the personal law, then the petitioners were told that even the challenges to the notice regime would not be heard, halfway through the Solicitor General's argument on the seventh day of the hearing. When mentioned at 2 p.m., the bench agreed to hear us on the issue, which was argued in rejoinder and then it was decided to leave the question open in the judgement a strange happenstance. Issues which have been argued at length in opening and in rejoinder, ought to have been answered one way or the other by the Court. I will critique the judgment at a later point in this book and will talk about it then. This is not the purpose of the chapter.

The difficulties and challenges that the queer movement faces in India are incredible. They are underscored by the flux in sociocultural impediments, legal issues and the shrinking space for dissent in the country today. Queer rights cannot be seen as divested from the broader clampdown on civil liberties by the Modi-led BJP government generally. Consider what happened with Kris Chudawala, an artist, designer and trans rights activist at Mumbai Pride. BJP leader Kirit Somaiya alleged that they had raised separatist slogans, and the police in retaliation slapped Kris and fifty others with sedition charges. In a virtual witch-hunt, Chudawala was deadnamed and trolled by right-wing accounts. Surprisingly, the organizers of the pride march, instead of rallying behind Chudawala, distanced themselves from the matter. What has also emerged since is that more and more pride parades are calling themselves *apolitical*, if such a thing can exist. These apolitical pride marches are little more than a night at a gay bar, full of fun and frolic, but of little meaning to the community itself. Queer identities involve negotiating with the State every day: Who can you marry, who can you live with, can you be criminalized. As a queer person, one has to negotiate equality in spite of the constitutional guarantee. With the Foreign Contribution Regulation Act (FCRA) noose being tightened around civil society and community-based organizations, there is also a dearth of funding that earlier used to come for HIV/AIDs which fuelled the initial days of queer rights movement before decriminalization. Majoritarian governments cannot be bothered with queer welfare; it is more convenient for them to whip up majoritarian sentiments and moral panic, dog whistle and project queers as the 'other'.

A shining example of this is the lack of funding for Garima Grehs, which are shelter homes for transgender persons, if they exist at all. These shelter homes also provide transgender persons with basic amenities like food, medical care and recreational facilities. The scheme also says that the government will release the grants at a 40–40–20 ratio (40 per cent at the initial stage, 40 per cent after six months of operation and 20 per cent at the end of the financial year). Notably, a massive state like Uttar Pradesh which also happens to be the state with the maximum number of transgender persons (approximately 1.37 lakh as per the 2011 census) does not have even a single Garima Greh. In the 2024-25 budget, the allocation for the 'Comprehensive Rehabilitation for Welfare of Transgender Persons' was increased from 52.91 crores in FY 24 to 68.46 crores. However, despite the allocation, only a fraction of it is actually utilized. For example, in FY 24, the utilized allocation was less than half at merely 22.82 crores. When there are no safe spaces for people to simply exist, how do we thrive?

The movement for queer liberation both inside and outside the court paints an incredibly intricate picture which would require another book by itself. How we went from being the 'minuscule minorities' in *Koushal* to being the 'urban elite' in *Supriyo* is surprising. Yet, irrespective of the labelling of queer persons, we have been systematically deprived of our rights, by the State, by society and our families. The only way that we thrive is if we are fighters. Who do I refer to when I say 'we'? If I can quote from the SPIT Manifesto,

We the sodomites. the perverts. the inverts. the faggots. the deviants. the queers, the keepers of spoiled identities, the tribadists, the promiscuous, the popper sniffing fist fuckers, the bottoms and the tops, the vers, the queens and the fairies, the nellies, the nancies and the fannies, the lady boys, the butch lesbians, the leather angels, the dykes, the daddies and the bulldaggers, the crossdressers and the drag queens, the auntie men, the Kikis, the trannies, the celesbians, the clones, the dykes on bikes, the sissies, the bone smugglers, the muscle marys, the jocks, the twinks, the bears and the otters, the sex pigs, the handballers, the gym queens, the hung, the carpet munchers, the pussy punchers, the fudge packers, the fruits, those who are light in the loafers, those who have sugar in the tank, the cocksuckers, the daffies, the friends of Dorothy, the bent, the poofs, the poofters, the buggers, the Uranians, the pillow biters, the sisters of Sappho, the silver foxes, the temperamental, the homophiles, the masters and the slaves, the tatted and pierced queens, the tightly-bound, the Lavender Menace, the pansies, the go-go boys, the hustlers, the trades, the chapstick lesbians, the lucky Pierres, the rough trades, the lacies, those who are queer as a three dollar bill, the mother superiors, the ring snatchers, the kissing fish, the tinkerbelles, the Ursulas, the vampires, the punks, the agfays, the ass bandits and the butt pirates, the beefcakes, the yard boys, the Zanies, the muff divers, the golden boys, the ten percenters, the sperm burpers, the boys in the band, the disordered, the dysfunctional, the diseased and the destructive, the bitches, those on the down low and the low down, the drag kings, the Tammies, the he-shes, the fishy girls, the cunts, the cut and the uncut, the bum bandits, the lipstick lesbians, the hard and the soft butches, the flamers, the gender benders, the butt huggers, the chicken hawks, the femme, the fuck boys, the gaylords, the masc for mases, the no pie no chats, the tranny chasers, the homos, the baby dykes, the gold stars, the gender queers, the pillow princesses, the studs, the bug chasers,

the barebackers, those who PnP, the campy queens, the
sword swallowers, the confirmed bachelors, the members
of a Boston marriage, the shims, those who read Playboy
for the articles, the Rosies, the people who are batting for
the other team, the AIDS carriers, the undetectables, the
pozzies, those on PrEP, the weak and morally sick wretches,
the deplorables, the sinners, the hedonists, those with the
aristocratic vice, those who enjoy the bourgeois decadence,
the Catamites and the Calamites, the cake eaters, the
chubby chasers, the midnight cowboys, the daffodils, the
fey, the Ganymedes, the limp-wristed, the salad tossers, the
ponces, those who are swishy, those of the reprobate mind,
the hermaphrodites, the chicks with dicks, the chemsexers,
the bearded ladies, the serodiscordants, the heartthrobs,
the theatrical types, the admirers, those who aren't 'clean',
the freaks, the cum guzzlers, the cumdumps, the tea
dancers, the momma's boys, the hot messes, the batty bois,
the degenerates . . .[22]

The *hijdas*, the *kothis*, the *chhakkas*, the *bailas*, the *aravanis* are
all the names that we call ourselves, or the names that we are
called. We are no longer going to be polite citizens. We are
no longer going to be the subject matter of political debates
without any agency ourselves. We resist being tolerated and
scream for acceptance and embraces. This is not because of
a largesse, but a demand for our rights as equal citizens in
society governed by a rule of law.

I do not wish to speak only of the law, for it will be myopic.
Nor do I speak of the law shrouded in legalese, and with
deference, as is the norm. The way I think and speak about
the law is fuelled by the pain of being told I am not equal, that
it is for an unbothered Parliament or a disinterested cabinet

secretary who is unbothered to decide what basic amenities I am entitled to, while their freedom is flaunted in our faces. This freedom is not expensive vacations or designer handbags that I speak of, but the right to live my daily life unbothered by State interference. I speak of the freedom of joint bank accounts, of marrying, of adopting children and of simply being myself. It comes from a place where I call upon my queer brothers, sisters and siblings, to arise, awaken and rest not until the constitutional promise of equality is fulfilled. The quest for equality, despite its grandiloquent claims and speeches made in Court or at political rallies, is about living your life without interference from the state or non-state actors. Rights are not given as largesse to any minority but are fought for and won. That is what I am going to do: Give a call for action. When the Supreme Court denies these rights, it contributes to a culture of inequality that kills people. It aids and abets the bullying of thousands of kids who are called names. It plays an active role in the murder and killing of transgender people. What else can you expect from a faggot like me? Not politeness, for sure. Because I am angry. Anger underlies this book, but it does not blind it. It is impossible to see constitutional law as devoid of emotion, and that is what makes the constitutional project meaningful.

Chapter 3

The Judicial Journey

The only reason they tolerated the transgender community in
some of these movements was because we were gung-ho, we were
front liners. We didn't take no shit from nobody. We had nothing
to lose. You all had rights. We had nothing to lose. I'll be the
first one to step on any organization, any politician's toes if
I have to, to get the rights for my community.
—Sylvia Rivera, *Street Transvestite Action Revolutionaries:*
Survival, Revolt, and Queer Antagonist Struggle[1]

When I started to write this chapter documenting the
history of queer struggles, the ideal way would have been to
trace the cases, from *Khairati* (the earliest legal reference to
queerness),[2] to *Naz*, to *Koushal*; from *NALSA* to *Puttuswamy*
and *Navtej*, and now *Supriyo*. But can a history of queer
struggle be written without talking about the bullying
faced by Arvey and Pranshu and their subsequent suicide,
Vyjayanti Vasanta Mogli's tireless activism to finally get the
Telangana Eunuch Act struck down or Grace Banu's fight
for horizontal reservations? Can the history of a movement
which is as diverse and as complex as the queer rights
movement be written in a linear format? Can it be seen

without foregrounding the movement in the vicissitudes of electoral politics, or without thinking about my own journey, both pre- and post-*Navtej?* The answer to this is no. And I go back to Oishik Sircar and Dipika Jain's piece, where they said:

> [W]hen a history of struggle is reduced to flashpoints like landmark judgments, it is a truncated, blinkered history that results in a sanitized politics that fossilises the past, valorises the present, and simply paints a clean picture: no contradictions, no contestations, no mess. A picture that irons out the unruly creases of historical inexplicability and is ready to adorn the manicured walls of an aesthetically curated memory museum.[3]

It is with this caveat that I suggest you read this chapter. It tells the tale of a few, and not all, struggles: Struggles that are known, and that have taken place in Delhi or in the Supreme Court. Thousands of queer people face the mighty State in India without access to legal resources for escaping violence, bullies, etc. They do not make it to the front pages of newspapers. They do not ever become known. I highlight selected cases here for only one reason: Legal clarity. A complex legal history will serve no other purpose than to complicate things. These cases are used only because Courts use precedent as a single answer from the majority opinions and judgements of larger benches. Law breeds conformity, and thus, it is important to know what we are conforming to.

I must state at the outset that I was involved with little, if any, queer activism until March 2021. I was not involved with legal fights until *Supriyo.* The deep and lonely recesses of the closet kept me away from not just activism, but for a long time, from acknowledging my own queerness. But broadly speaking, the movement has changed its course in the courts. The fight began with the tireless activism of the AIDS Bhedbhav Virodhi Andolan (ABVA) consisting of left-wing folks from the medical, legal, academic, human rights and social work fields. In April 1994, the ABVA filed the first petition running into hundreds of pages in the Delhi High Court, asking for Section 377, which criminalized homosexuality, to be struck down. The petition arose out of the need for condoms for men having sex with men (MSM) which was opposed by Tihar Jail authorities, headed by Kiran Bedi. The petition asked for the following prayers:

a. To declare that Section 377 of the Indian Penal Code is unconstitutional and void as being hit by the provisions of Articles 13, 14 and 21 and 25 of the Constitution of India;

b. To direct the implementation of the government's national AIDS program;

c. To declare that all action and proceedings purporting to have been done or taken by the respondents and each of them under the said unconstitutional and void laws are wholly unauthorized by law, illegal and void and not binding on the jail inmates;

d. To restrain the respondents from segregating or isolating prisoners with a certain sexual orientation or those suffering from AIDS or from commencing prosecution against those prisoners who are suspected to have participated in consensual anal intercourse;

e. To direct the respondents to immediately make condoms available at the dispensary within Tihar Jail, where prisoners can freely obtain them without fear that they will be persecuted on account of their sexual orientation;

f. To direct that only disposable syringes be used in the dispensary within Tihar Jail;

g. To direct the jail authorities to regularly consult with the National AIDS Control Organisation, namely the Respondent No. 6;

h. May pass any other writ, direction or order as this Hon'ble Court deems fit and proper in the circumstances of this case.

In January 2001, the ABVA became defunct, and the matter was dismissed as no lawyer appeared in the matter for the petitioner.

Three years before this litigation, for the first time, in 1991, the ABVA had come out with the first Indian queer manifesto titled 'Less than Gay: A Citizens' Report on the Status of Homosexuality in India' that laid out a charter of queer rights in India including same-sex marriage. Decades later, in 2022, the ABVA came out with a second edition of the same report, detailing its struggle since 1988–89 for the full repeal of Section 377. The organization's work is often overlooked in the public discourse but it is so overarching that it finds mention even in *Supriyo*, albeit only in a footnote. The first report, which ran into seventy pages and was dedicated to 'the numerous gaymen [sic] and lesbians who shared their intimate experiences, fears, and longings', had a charter of demands which perhaps was way ahead of its time. It called upon the Government of India to:

1. Repeal all discriminatory legislation singling out homosexual acts by consenting adults in private—

Section 377 of the Indian Penal Code, and the relevant sections of the Army, Navy and Air Force Acts, 1950. In other words, decriminalize sodomy;

2. Enact civil rights legislation to offer gay citizens and other sexual minorities such as hijras the same protections now guaranteed to others on the basis of caste, creed and colour. Amend the Constitution to include equality before the law on the basis of 'sex' and 'sexual orientation';

3. Recognize the right to privacy as a fundamental part of the citizen's right to life and liberty, including the right to his or her sexual orientation;

4. Reform police policy (for example, by calling a meeting of senior police officers, including all station house officers [SHOs]), to put an end to the harassment of gay people at the hands of the police and the public. Police authorities should take the initiative to make available information on all local public nuisance laws used on gay people in public places, and the relevant procedures and penalties specified therein. They should also make public the numbers of arrests, prosecutions and convictions of gay people under various laws along with the period of sentence, amount of fine and age of the offenders;

5. Establish a commission to document human rights violations of gay people, such as violence and blackmail directed at gay men and lesbians, as well as atrocities within marriage on lesbians who may be married to men;

6. Redefine the offence of rape in the Indian Penal Code to include all coercive sexual acts rather than only vaginal penetration. Rape laws should be made

applicable to both men and women, irrespective of whether they are gay, nongay, married or single;

7. Have the Press Council of India issue guidelines for respectful, sensitive and representative reporting on gay men and lesbians and issues around homosexuality;

8. Have the Medical Council of India (MCI) issue guidelines to the effect that [the] refusal to treat a person on the basis of his/her sexual orientation is a cause for censure on grounds of professional misconduct. Bring medical curricula in schools and medical colleges in line with the latest scientific theories of homosexuality;

9. Consider unethical any reckless and uncalled-for sex change surgery without informed consent and counselling. Counselling should be made available to help a person deal with the normality of his/her gender incongruities. Any irresponsible experimentation by medical professionals in this area should be made punishable by law;

10. Institute a massive, nationwide survey of sexual behaviour in our society;

11. Ensure that everyone receives judgement-free health education related to sexuality, homosexuality, sexually transmitted diseases (STDs), HIV testing, AIDS and condom use. All AIDS-related education should explicitly acknowledge sexual interaction between people of the same sex;

12. Delete the clauses in the AIDS (Prevention) Bill, 1989 (which lies pending before a Joint Parliamentary Committee) that provide for coercive testing, contact tracing and isolation. Include explicit confidentiality on sexual orientation and anti-discrimination measures for the protection of people with HIV/AIDS;

13. Make available anonymous HIV testing facilities for all;
14. Alter the heterosexist bias in education, from school onwards, by presenting positive images and role models of gay men and lesbians and of homosexuality as a viable, healthy alternative lifestyle;
15. Amend the Special Marriage Act to allow for marriages between people of the same sex (or between people who may be intersexed, or have undergone sex-change surgery and any others). All consequential legal benefits of marriage should extend to gay marriages as well, including the right to adopt children, to execute a partner's will, to inherit, etc. Same-sex couples should also be entitled to the legal benefits that accrue to their heterosexual counterparts of common-law marriages. No presumption as to fitness or unfitness for custody of mild or visitation rights shall arise based on the sexual orientation of either parent in such a situation.
16. Alternatively, legally recognize and encourage friendship agreements between single people of the same sex as a valid way of organizing family life.[4]

This was perhaps quite a radical document of its time—since 1991, we have succeeded in achieving a few of these aims, had limited success in others and completely failed in some of them. The successes, of course, include the repeal of Section 377 (though the analogous provisions in the Army, Navy and Air Force Acts remain on the statute books) and the right to privacy. We have an HIV anti-discrimination legislation, though implementation remains a difficult task on the ground. Tackling police violence, eliminating medical discrimination, advocating for marriage equality and friendship arrangements (now rechristened in popular discourse as 'chosen families') still remain distant dreams. But ABVA's fight did not end in 1989.

In 2022, the Andolan's second report was much more exhaustive, running into 213 pages. This report talked about not just the struggles of the ABVA itself, but also of individual members. It had no funding, no office. It had members ranging from twenty-four years old to fifty-five years old who ranged from residents of some of Delhi's poshest colonies to pavement-dwellers. Their activism was one of the main forces behind making sure that the AIDS (Prevention) Bill, 1989, which allowed, inter alia, the isolation, forcible testing and questioning of people who were living with HIV with no provision in place which ensured the protection of confidentiality was tabled in Parliament. But here is some trivia, which even I learnt after reading the second ABVA report during the course of the research for this book: Dr S. Muralidhar, who later became Justice Muralidhar, appeared for the ABVA in its first petition. Later on, Muralidhar would go on to become a judge, and be a part of the bench that would for the first time, in 2009, strike down Section 377 as being violative of Articles 14, 15 and 21, along with Justice A.P. Shah. This was, in my mind, the first phase of the fight for queer rights, a phase that was focused on combating HIV/AIDS and was dictated by the carnal act of sex.

In the second part of this journey that I will now talk about, that is, Naz Foundation and Ors v. Suresh Kumar Koushal and Anr in the Delhi High Court, the issue had become about the identity of queer individuals, namely, MSM (men who have sex with men) and gay men. The popular discourses around Section 377, much of the work focuses on gay men and MSM. This process, in my mind, erases the tireless work done by trans, hijra, kothi persons, sex workers, people from the working class, Dalit, Bahujan and Adivasi persons. Trans petitioners were, even during *Navtej*, used merely for checking off a DEI (diversity, equity and inclusion) box.

But now we come to 2 July 2009, and the judgment in the Naz Foundation case. There were two legal teams that took on Section 377 this time, successfully: The first led by Anil Diwan and the second led by Anand Grover. A division bench of Justices A.P. Shah and Muralidhar struck down Section 377 as being violative of Articles 14, 15, 19 and 21 of the Constitution of India. But before that, what was this Section 377? Section 377 of the IPC (the erstwhile criminal code of India) was contained in Chapter XVI of the IPC titled 'Of Offences Affecting the Human Body'. The offence was categorized under the sub-chapter titled 'Of Unnatural Offences. It read as follows:

> 377. Unnatural Offences: Whoever voluntarily has carnal intercourse against the order of nature with any man, woman or animal, shall be punished with imprisonment for life, or with imprisonment of either description for a term which may extend to ten years, and shall also be liable to fine.
>
> Explanation: Penetration is sufficient to constitute the carnal intercourse necessary to the offence described in this section.

Simply put, the section criminalized non-penal-vaginal sexual intercourse. However, it was used extensively against gay men and transgender persons by the police, into demanding forced sex, extortion and dehumanization. One such instance, amongst others, is used by the judges in the judgment. In paragraph 22, the judgment notes:

The victim of the torture was a hijra (eunuch) from Bangalore, who was at a public place dressed in female clothing. The person was subjected to gang rape, forced to have oral and anal sex by a group of hooligans. He was later taken to [the] police station where he was stripped naked, handcuffed to the window, grossly abused and tortured merely because of his sexual identity.

This is a systematic process of dehumanization which continues to this day and was eloquently highlighted in the arguments of Jayna Kothari who appeared for Akkai Padmashali in *Supriyo* and by Raju Ramachandran who appeared for Kajal to rebut the Union's assertion that queerness is an urban elite concept. I will talk about this in the part of the book. Notably, the word 'love' which dominated much of the discourse in *Navtej* is not even mentioned once in the judgment. I was merely a child who did not even know what queerness was then. So I have no recollection of the memories of those days. I think it is best to rely then on those who were there to speak about the judgment. Kajal Bharadwaj, in her piece for the *Asian Age*, speaks of the day that the judgment was delivered. She writes:

It was expected. Yet when these words were read out, 'We declare that Section 377 IPC, insofar it criminalizes consensual sexual acts of adults in private, is violative of Articles 21, 14 and 15 of the Constitution', an audible gasp went around the room. By the time the Chief Justice had finished reading the conclusion of the judgment, people were openly weeping and there were handshakes and hugs all around.

Watching the spectators collapse on each other, overcome by emotion, the guards charged with maintaining decorum in the court room quickly ushered the group out.

Out of the court room and down three floors, most walked in a daze, looking around at their friends and colleagues wondering if they had actually heard what they had been waiting to hear for so long. Other lawyers in the Delhi high court gaped at the big troop descending the stairs, one wondering out loud with unintentional accuracy, '*Kahan se release hoke aayen hain ye sab* (Where have all these people been released from)?'[5]

In their judgment, which runs into over 100 pages, Justices Shah and Muralidhar ground their arguments in four principles: dignity, privacy, equality and non-discrimination. Adopting, for the first time, a topic that is now much in debate, that of constitutional morality, the judges held that popular morality is not a valid ground to curtail fundamental rights under Article 21. They relied on a passage in Menaka Gandhi v. Union of India which also succinctly tells us why the judgment in *Supriyo* is wrong. In *Menaka Gandhi*, Justice Krishna Iyer, one of our finest judges, wrote:

> The compulsion of constitutional humanism and the assumption of full faith in life and liberty cannot be so futile or fragmentary that any transient legislative majority in tantrums against any minority, by three quick readings of a bill with the requisite quorum, can prescribe any unreasonable modality and thereby sterilise the grandiloquent mandate.

But the joy of the community after the victory in *Naz Foundation* was short-lived. Appeals were immediately filed before the Supreme Court seeking to overrule the decision. There was a strange mix of parties which appealed: Hindu,

Muslim and Christian fundamentalists who otherwise agreed on little mounted a legal challenge to the verdict. These were the days before the live-streaming, transcribing and live-tweeting of court proceedings, and it would be apposite at this juncture to pay tribute to the lawyers who documented the whole case. Reading the transcript of the case, which has been compiled by Orinam, makes one seethe. Look at the exchange below, which I replicate from the transcripts created by Orinam, which has become perhaps the most infamous exchange in the *Koushal* hearings, and one that guided the decision that the bench made:

'Mr Malhotra, by the way, nothing to do with the case, but do you know any person who is homosexual?' asked Justice Singhvi.

Mr Malhotra continued to read from the written submissions.

'You are avoiding our question,' said Justice Singhvi. 'You don't know anybody?' he asked.

'I must confess my ignorance about modern society,' said Mr Malhotra.

'We appreciate your ignorance,' joked Justice Singhvi.

This mockery which was made of queer lives continues to this day, inside courtrooms, in the corridors of the courts, in law firms and in other settings. A striking example of this, during the hearings in *Supriyo*, was the Solicitor General reading out various 'types of genders' from a random website, which included a gender identity that had people 'changing gender according to mood swings'. This is of course homophobia disguised as legal language. But the reason for this is slightly more complex: The law, at its core, seeks to regulate and bring order to chaos. So, when the law is faced with something like queerness, which is amorphous, which obfuscates boundaries, the desire of lawyers to ensure conformity feels threatened. Queerness is love and freedom in their purest forms, unhindered and unbothered. It is new, it is impossible. It grows out of a struggle, it requires fighting—you need to be a fighter if you are queer and want to survive. The law cannot contain queerness. That is why the law and lawyers are scared of queerness and the havoc it will wreak on their desire for conformity.

One year and eight months after the oral arguments in Suresh Kumar Koushal were concluded, and on the day Justice Singhvi was about to retire, the judgment was pronounced. On 11 December 2013, the court held that persons from the LGBTQ+ community were a 'minuscule minority' and did not deserve the protection of the law or the Constitution. 'In view of the above discussion, we hold that Section 377 IPC does not suffer from the vice of unconstitutionality and the declaration made by the Division Bench of the high court is legally unsustainable.' With these words, the division bench of the Supreme Court threw the lives of thousands of queer Indians into chaos and declared their love to be unconstitutional. Like the judgment in *Supriyo*, the bench also noted that it was within the realm of Parliament to debate and decide on repealing Section 377.

In January 2014, on the heels of this decision, Justice Leila Seth, one of the first women judges of the High Court of Delhi and the mother of famous author Vikram Seth, wrote a scathing op-ed in the *Times of India*. She minced no words, writing:

What makes life meaningful is love. The right that makes us human is the right to love. To criminalize the expression of that right is profoundly cruel and inhumane. To acquiesce in such criminalization or, worse, to recriminalize it, is to display the very opposite of compassion. To show exaggerated deference to a majoritarian Parliament when the matter is one of fundamental rights is to display judicial pusillanimity, for there is no doubt, that in the constitutional scheme, it is the judiciary that is the ultimate interpreter.[6]

The community was shocked, and the motto 'No going back' became a recurrent theme at pride marches in post-*Koushal* India. Eight review petitions were filed: Union of India, Naz Foundation, Voices against 377, Minna Saran and eighteen other parents (together in one petition), Dr Shekhar Seshadri and thirteen other mental health professionals, Nivedita Menon and fifteen other academics and Shyam Benegal. They were dismissed by a division bench of the Supreme Court consisting of Justices Dattu and Mukhopadhyay. Curative petitions were filed by seven parties in April 2013, and the court agreed to hear the curative petitions in the open on 14 April. Nothing came of this. In the meantime, the abuse of Section 377 and queer persons by the police continued. The community was thrown back into the closet by the court. But there was 'no going back'.

* * *

In the meantime, on 15 April 2015, a division bench of the Supreme Court which had heard the petitions filed by NALSA, Lakshmi Narayan Tripathi and others delivered the judgment in NALSA v. Union of India. 'Recognition of transgenders as a third gender is not a social or medical issue but a human rights issue,' said Justice Radhakrishnan while delivering the judgment. It allowed transgender individuals to identify themselves as the third gender, or to transition to another gender. It also directed both the Union of India and the state governments to grant legal recognition to them. Coming as it did on the heels of the judgment in *Koushal*, *NALSA* was quite strange. As Danish Sheikh writes, the judgment holds that transgender persons, 'even though they were insignificant in numbers, were still human beings and therefore they have every right to enjoy their human rights'.[7] Recognizing the vulnerability of transgender persons and the misuse of Section 377 against hijra, kothi and transgender persons, the court held that discrimination on the grounds of gender identity and sexual orientation violated Articles 14, 15 and 21 of the Constitution of India. Another significant finding of the court was that a right against discrimination on the basis of sex under Article 15 extended 'to prevent the direct or indirect attitude to treat people differently, for the reason of not being in conformity with stereotypical generalizations of binary genders'. It laid down several guidelines for transgender persons:

1. Hijras, eunuchs, apart from binary gender, be treated as 'third gender' for the purpose of safeguarding their rights under Part III of our Constitution and the laws made by the Parliament and the State Legislature.
2. Transgender persons' right to decide their self-identified gender is also upheld and the Centre and State Governments are directed to grant legal recognition of their gender identity such as male, female or third gender.

3. We direct the Centre and the state governments to take steps to treat them as socially and educationally backward classes of citizens and extend all kinds of reservation in cases of admission in educational institutions and for public appointments.

4. Centre and state governments are directed to operate separate HIV sero-surveillance centres since hijras/transgenders face several sexual health issues.

5. Centre and state governments should seriously address the problems being faced by Hijras/Transgenders such as fear, shame, gender dysphoria, social pressure, depression, suicidal tendencies, social stigma, etc. and any insistence for SRS [sex reassignment surgery] for declaring one's gender is immoral and illegal.

6. Centre and state governments should take proper measures to provide medical care to TGs in the hospitals and also provide them separate public toilets and other facilities.

7. Centre and state governments should also take steps to frame various social welfare schemes for their betterment.

8. Centre and state governments should take steps to create public awareness so that TGs will feel that they are also part and parcel of the social life and be not treated as untouchables.

9. Centre and state governments should also take measures to regain their respect and place in the society which once they enjoyed in our cultural and social life.

The judgment took judicial cognizance of the fact that transgender persons were faced with 'extreme discrimination in all spheres of society' which was a violation of their constitutional right to equality. Further, the court held that Article 19(1)(a) of the Constitution which provided for freedom of speech and expression included the right to expression of gender, 'through dress, words, action, or behaviour'. Radhakrishnan J's opinion also talked about providing reservations to transgender persons under Article 15(4) and Article 16(4) of the Constitution of India. This is the issue that the community is still grappling with: Campaigns for horizontal reservations now have taken some form across India, and even made it to the manifesto of a few political parties in the run-up to the 2024 elections.

Though *NALSA* was hailed as a liberal judgment, it had its own fair share of criticisms. Justice Sikri's opinion was also riddled with stereotyping transgender persons and laced with latent queerphobia. Consider this passage from his opinion, 'Obviously transvestites, the hijra beg from merchants who quickly, under threat of obscene abuse, respond to the silent demands of such detested individuals. On occasion, especially festival days, they press their claims with boisterous and ribald singing and dancing.' Another shortcoming was that Justice Sikri, in his opinion, held that the decision is limited to the communities identified in the judgment and the reference to 'transgender' is thus restricted to the communities identified in the judgment. The communities were the hijras, kothis, *shiva-shaktis*, aravanis and *jogappas*. Santa Khurrai, one of the fiercest advocates for indigenous trans communities, has been a vocal critic of this. Santa is a Nupi Manabi activist from Manipur. She has long held the view that this judgment did nothing for indigenous trans communities which were not brought to the attention of the court. If Justice Sikri's opinion[8] is taken, then what happens to trans men, to non-binary individuals, to agender people?

This brings me to what I was saying earlier: the law is a tool of conformity. Queerness defies conformity. Law and queerness will, thus, always be in conflict. Since the NALSA judgment, there have been multiple attempts to secure the rights of transgender persons through statutes in 2014, 2015, 2016, 2018 and 2019. It was only the 2019 statute which became an Act of Parliament, and the rules that were notified in 2020 that have the force of law. All of these bills sought to provide rights to transgender persons, yet not only were the rights different, but so were the people they sought to bring under their ambit.

Let us look at how each of these bills defined a transgender person:

2014 bill: 'Transgender person' means a person whose gender does not match with the gender assigned to that person at birth and includes trans-men and trans-women (whether or not they have undergone sex reassignment surgery or hormone therapy or laser therapy, etc.), gender-queers and a number of socio-cultural identities such as—kinnars, hijras, aravanis, jogtas, etc.

2015 bill: 'Transgender person' means a person whose gender does not match with the gender assigned to that person at birth and includes trans-men and trans-women (whether or not they have undergone sex reassignment surgery or hormone therapy or laser therapy, etc.), gender-queers and a number of socio-cultural identities such as—kinnars, hijras, aravanis, jogtas, etc. A transgender person should have the option to choose either 'man', 'woman' or 'transgender' as well as have the right to choose any of the options independent of surgery/hormones.

2016 bill (as introduced in the Lok Sabha): 'Transgender person' means a person who is—

(A) neither wholly female nor wholly male; or

(B) a combination of female or male; or

(C) neither female nor male;

and whose sense of gender does not match with the gender assigned to that person at the time of birth, and includes trans-men and trans-women, persons with intersex variations and gender-queers.

2018 bill: 'Transgender person' means a person whose gender does not match with the gender assigned to that person at birth and includes trans-man or trans-woman (whether or not such person has undergone Sex Reassignment Surgery or hormone therapy or laser therapy or such other therapy), person with intersex variations, gender-queer and person having such socio-cultural identities as kinner, hijra, aravani and jogta.

2019 Act: 'Transgender person' means a person whose gender does not match with the gender assigned to that person at birth and includes trans-man or trans-woman (whether or not such person has undergone sex reassignment surgery or hormone therapy or laser therapy or such other therapy), person with intersex variations, genderqueer and person having such socio-cultural identities as kinner, hijra, aravani and jogta.

Notably, all the bills as well as the present Act have come under vehement community criticism. Like all bills and Acts that are passed these days, these were drafted without or with little community consultations, and effectively put the right of self-determination in the hands of a government officer. I do not propose to go into the criticism of each bill or its salient features here. I will, however, focus on the 2019 Act ('trans act') since it has become the law. *NALSA* had held that the right to self-determination is a part of the fundamental right to life of a transgender person, but the 2019 bill disallowed it. A person's transness is only valid in the eyes of the state if there is a certification issued by the government under Sections 6 and 7 of the Trans Act. There is a huge backlog in issuing transgender ID cards, lack of trans-affirmative government employees, lack of standard operating procedures, stigma, defunct portals and innumerable psychiatric and medical tests which must be undergone to get the state to *certify* one's transness. The Trans Act also denied the right to reservation that *NALSA* had promised. The constitutional validity of the Act is under challenge in the Supreme Court, but it is yet to be taken up despite multiple pleas which have been filed. How does one define queerness? Each person defines their queerness for themselves. However, sometimes, such as when seeking legal protections or reservations, it is important and perhaps even unavoidable to define queerness. That is what leads to these troubles.

* * *

Much after *NALSA*, there was a flurry of judgments of Constitution benches in the Supreme Court. Two judgements of note were the judgments of Justice K.S. Puttaswamy, of a nine-judge Constitution bench which recognized the right to privacy, and the Navtej Singh Johar judgment, which decriminalized homosexuality.

These two judgments warrant a deep dive for two reasons for the purposes of this book: First, they were repeatedly referred to in *Supriyo*, and second, without understanding the contours of the rights laid down by the Supreme Court, it becomes legally impossible to understand how the Supreme Court faltered in *Supriyo*.

The origins of *Puttaswamy* were hardly related to queer rights. In 2012, Justice K.S. Puttaswamy, a retired high court judge, filed a writ petition in the Supreme Court challenging the constitutional validity of the Aadhaar scheme which was introduced by the United Progressive Alliance (UPA) government.

But how does a case get referred to nine judges? The Supreme Court has thirty-four judges who sit in a combination of two or three on a usual day. There are a few basic rules: The decision of a larger bench is binding on a bench of lesser strength. However, a bench of a smaller size can doubt the correctness of a larger bench's decision and refer it to an even larger bench. This can happen in two ways: Either the case works its way through the system from two judges to three to five and so on, or the Chief Justice with his power as a Master of the Roster refers the matter to a larger bench directly. When this matter came up before a bench of three judges comprising Justices J. Chelameswar, S.A. Bobde and C. Nagappan, they passed an order directing that a bench of appropriate strength must examine the correctness of the decisions in M.P. Sharma v. Satish Chandra,[9] district magistrate, Delhi, which was an eight-judge bench decision, and Kharak Singh v. State of Uttar Pradesh,[10] which was a six-judge bench decision that held that the right to privacy was not a fundamental right. At the core of this reference order was whether the right to privacy is a fundamental right under the Indian Constitution. The Puttaswamy case was first placed before a five-judge bench headed by the incumbent Chief Justice, Justice J. Khehar, who referred it to a nine-judge Bench on 18 July 2017. The Bench comprised (in the order of seniority) Chief Justice Khehar and Justices J. Chelameswar, S.A. Bobde, D.Y. Chandrachud, Abdul Nazeer, R.F. Nariman, R.K. Agarwal, Abhay Manohar Sapre and Sanjay Kishan Kaul. Arguments began on 19 July 2017 and concluded on 2 August 2017.

The Puttaswamy judgment ran into hundreds of pages. It dealt with a range of issues, from constitutional values to liberty, from fundamental rights to limits of state interference. There were six opinions, of which the majority opinion was written by Justice Chandrachud for himself, Chief Justice Khehar and Justices Agrawal and Nazeer. Justices Sapre, Nariman, Bobde, Kaul and Chelameswar wrote their own judgments. Two of these nine judges in *Puttaswamy* (Justices Kaul and Chandrachud) were present in the *Supriyo* case—they formed the minority opinion.

I refer, in this analysis, to only the relevant portions of the judgment which have a direct bearing on how we understand marriage equality in terms of how the court understood not just the right to privacy but also fundamental rights. All nine judges agreed that there was a fundamental right to privacy under Article 21 of the Constitution which protects life and liberty.

The majority opinion authored by Justice Chandrachud and Justice Kaul warrants a deep dive: an analysis of their opinions and their juxtaposition to the marriage equality judgment will show how their minority opinions cannot stand scrutiny in the face of their own judgments in *Puttaswamy*.

Justice Chandrachud's opinion and his judgment are the law as laid down by the Supreme Court since he wrote it on behalf of the majority. First, he held that constitutional interpretation and the demands that we place on the Constitution must evolve to meet the challenges of the times we live in. Second, he went on to say that every individual, irrespective of his social or economic status, is entitled by virtue of his right to privacy, to intimacy and autonomy. Third, he further held that privacy coexists with a person's liberty and right to exercise control over his own personality. Finally, he held that the right to privacy recognizes the ability of each individual to control crucial decisions that affect his life, and safeguards the autonomy exercised in matters of 'personal intimacies, matters of home and marriage, the sanctity of family life and sexual orientation, all of which are at the core of privacy'.[11] His opinion in *Puttaswamy* had practically overruled *Koushal*. In paragraph 127 of his judgment, he wrote:

> The view in *Koushal* that the High Court had erroneously relied upon international precedents 'in its anxiety to protect the so-called rights of LGBT. persons' is similarly, in our view, unsustainable. The rights of the lesbian, gay, bisexual and transgender population cannot be construed to be 'so-called rights'. The expression 'so-called' seems to suggest the exercise of a liberty in the garb of a right which is illusory. This is an inappropriate construction of the privacy based claims of the LGBT population. Their rights are not 'so-called' but are real rights founded on sound constitutional doctrine. They inhere in the right to life. They dwell in privacy and dignity. They constitute the essence of liberty and freedom. Sexual orientation is an essential component of identity. Equal protection demands protection of the identity of every individual without discrimination.

Justice Kaul made a powerful case in his opinion for protecting individual choices. He wrote, 'The right of privacy is a fundamental right. It is a right which protects the inner sphere of the individual from interference from both State, and non-State actors and allows the individuals to make autonomous life choices.' He further said that civil liberties of past, present and future must be read into the Constitution. Protecting the right to decisional autonomy, he opined that it is the very hallmark of freedom in a democracy. Notably, he took a dig at the 'minuscule minority' jurisprudence of *Koushal* and held that simply because a minuscule fraction of the population is impacted by the infringement of a fundamental right, the said right cannot be denied. Justice Kaul in a post-retirement interview confessed that was the judge who presided over the bench of the Delhi High Court which issued a notice in the first case against Section 377 in 2001.[12] Holding that sexual autonomy must be an essential attribute of privacy, he wrote, 'It is an individual's choice as to who enters his house, how he lives and in what relationship. The privacy of the home must protect the family, marriage, procreation and sexual orientation which are all important aspects of dignity.'

Justice Chelameswar held that to realize liberty in its truest sense, privacy is essential. He opined that privacy incorporates three aspects: Repose, sanctuary and intimate decision. Intimate decision, as Anand Grover, whom I was briefing, argued in our petition as a right to intimate association, was not accepted by the majority in *Supriyo*. For infringement of privacy, Chelameswar held, the strictest scrutiny standard of compelling state interest must be used. To a certain extent, Justice Bobde also agreed with this proposition and held that the right to privacy entailed both a positive as well as a negative autonomy to do or not do a specific act.

Justice Nariman's opinion held that privacy begins where liberty ends. He held that the right to privacy included the right to be free from interference—he held that it must be developed on a case-to-case basis since all of its contours could not be laid down in a single case, given the amorphous nature of the right. Justice Sapre's opinion held that the right to privacy was essential to lead a meaningful and dignified life.

Once privacy was read in the Constitution, and with the scathing comments on *Koushal* in the majority opinion as well as the opinion of Justice Kaul, the lawyers who challenged Section 377 in *Navtej* were practically on a winning wicket, a game that they were bound to win. Curative petitions challenging the decision in *Koushal* were still pending, as I wrote earlier, but fresh challenges were mounted by five individuals challenging the constitutional validity of Section 377 insofar as it criminalized same-sex activities between consenting adults. This was the final phase of the fight against Section 377, where the debates had moved to love. Mind you, it was still about HIV, identity and the disproportionate impact of Section 377 on queer and trans people. Vqueeram and Akhil Kang have, in their discussion, talked about the erasure of trans and Dalit petitioners. Vqueeram said:

> However, it is not as if kothis and trans folx disappear from the petitions, they continue to remain in petitions as evidence of the social violence of the law. But they are not represented in the courtrooms. The petition becomes the place where you have the social life of the law, which seems regressive and backward, and those who represent it and the petitioners become the harbingers of futurity. Stigma, social violence and state atrocity get pushed to the back of the room, become a matter of history, become a matter of the past; while conversations about respect and 'equal love' become matters of the future. The word 'shame' appears about five times in the five hundred pages of the judgement,

and is replaced by the word 'prejudice', which appears about seventy times or more in comparison. This turn from shame to prejudice is important to point out: Prejudice is that which you can overcome, while shame is that which continues to debilitate you, continues to affect the future. You cannot overcome shame in the same way—especially not through the law. This is why the trans, kothi and sex workers who inhabit shame and stigma as marks on their body are not brought in to the courtroom. People who can hold the future, who can become the future, are brought to the courtroom instead. These are the most respectable of us, those who look most like the judges themselves.[13]

This is a critique that lays bare who gets represented in the courtroom, what stories are told in court which masquerade as legal strategy. Legal strategy often comes at the cost of erasure.

But I come back to Section 377. On 5 January, a five-judge bench was constituted to hear the challenge to its validity. The bench consisted of Chief Justice Dipak Misra, Justice A.M. Khanwilkar, Justice D.Y. Chandrachud, Justice R.F. Nariman and Justice Indu Malhotra. The decision came on 6 September 2018 and decriminalized same-sex consensual intercourse with four judgments: Justice Misra writing for himself and Justice Khanwilkar; Justices Chandrachud, Nariman and Malhotra writing their own decisions. Given the nature of the arguments, the hearings did not take long and got over in a matter of four days.

All four judgments held that the reading of Section 377 was a violation of fundamental rights against the queer community on the basis of their gender identity, sexual orientation or gender identity. This, they ruled, violates Article 14, which provides for equal protection of the law and equality before the law, and Article 15 which prohibits discrimination on the basis of sex, place of birth, etc. All five judges ruled that Section 377 violated the rights to life, dignity and autonomy of personal choice as read in *Puttaswamy* under Article 21. Finally, all judges held that the right to sexual orientation is protected by Article 19(1)(a) of the Constitution. There are, however, some differences in the way each judge looks at why Section 377 is unconstitutional.

Chief Justice Misra wrote a judgment on behalf of himself and Justice Khanwilkar. He began it with Goethe's famous adage of, 'I am as I am. So take me as I am.' These lines have now stuck to defining what the judgment was about. It emphasized an individual's right to self-determination which drew on decisional autonomy and privacy. Much of his judgment was focused on protecting personal intimacy and autonomy for sexual orientation. Section 377, in his judgment, was held unconstitutional on both tests under Article 14 of the Constitution for holding a law unconstitutional: 'Manifest arbitrariness', which allows a court to strike down any law on the ground of it being capricious or irrational. He further held that the failure to meet the 'reasonable classification test'. What does this mean? Under our equality jurisprudence, the State only has to treat like as like, and unlike as unlike. The State can discriminate against citizens if it proves that such discrimination is based on intelligible differentia or a reasoned difference. Such a distinction must also have a nexus to the cause that the discrimination seeks to achieve. He held that any veil, including that of social morality, cannot be weaponized against even a single individual so as to violate his fundamental rights. He stressed that the foundation of constitutional morality was characterized by the appreciation of diversity that ran through the Constitution.

Justice Chandrachud's opinion was as poetic as it was jurisprudentially strong. Calling Section 377 an 'anachronistic colonial law', he said that the right to sexual orientation was an important contour of the right to privacy which had been read into fundamental rights under Article 21 as recognized in *Puttuswamy*. In his judgment, he noted that males and females are not binary biological categories. The same remark, when made during the marriage equality case, drew a lot of vitriol on social media. Justice Chandrachud was bitterly—and in my opinion, unfairly—trolled. Calling for a transformative constitutionalism which moves on with the times, he held that the decriminalization of homosexuality was only a necessary *first step* on the path to guaranteeing queer individuals their constitutional rights. The parting words in his decision are quite prophetic, and deserve a reiteration:

> The ability of a society to acknowledge the injustices which it has perpetuated is a mark of its evolution. In the process of remedying wrongs under a regime of constitutional remedies, recrimination gives way to restitution, diatribes pave the way for dialogue and healing replaces the hate of a community. For those who have been oppressed, justice under a regime committed to human freedom, has the power to transform lives. In addressing the causes of oppression and injustice, society transforms itself. The Constitution has within it the ability to produce a social catharsis. The importance of this case lies in telling us that reverberations of how we address social conflict in our times will travel far beyond the narrow alleys in which they are explored.

Justice Nariman wrote a forensic judgment, tracing the history of the sodomy and buggery laws in England and other

Commonwealth countries. On the eve of the hearings, the Indian Psychiatric Association had put out a statement that homosexuality is not a disease. Using the provisions of the Mental Healthcare Act, Justice Nariman recognized and declared that homosexuality is not a disease. His judgment primarily held that the distinction between carnal intercourse against the order of nature, that is, unnatural sex and natural sex was manifestly arbitrary and thus in violation of Article 14. The final part of the judgment passed the following guidelines to ameliorate the stigma and discomfiture of society against homosexual persons:

> We are also of the view that the Union of India shall take all measures to ensure that this judgment is given wide publicity through the public media, which includes television, radio, print and online media at regular intervals, and initiate programs to reduce and finally eliminate the stigma associated with such persons. Above all, all government officials, including and in particular police officials, and other officers of the Union of India and the States, be given periodic sensitization and awareness training of the plight of such persons in the light of the observations contained in this judgment.

Before the court was supposed to hear the Marriage Equality Case, Akhilesh Godi, one of the IITians who was a petitioner, filed a Right to Information (RTI) application with at least five ministries, including the Ministry of Law and Justice, which was a respondent in *Navtej* about whether or not the ministry had given publicity to the judgment as directed by Justice Nariman. Unsurprisingly, either no work was done, or in some cases, the file had gone missing.[14]

Justice Indu Malhotra spoke about historical wrongs against the LGBTQ community, and how society owed them an apology. In so many ways, her judgment was about historical wrongs and the historical perception of the LGBTQ community. She spoke extensively about the disproportionate impact of HIV/AIDS on the queer community, and how that results in violation of the right to health. She wrote about stigma, the fear of living in the closet and how it affects queer people. She traced the apology issued by Theresa May, the British Prime Minister, spoke about the anti-sodomy laws, and ended her concurring opinion with a powerful line, 'The LGBT persons deserve to live a life unshackled from the shadow of being "unapprehended felons."'

* * *

I was born in 1998. I was coming of age around the time of *NALSA*. I had known I was queer; having a crush on a classmate, seeing boys in my dreams, being jeered and mocked in school, and sometimes physical violence. Thankfully, the bullying never turned sexual. I remember one particular incident: Sometime around 2014, I told another male classmate that that day was Valentine's Day. He went and complained that I had wished him a Happy Valentine's Day—and I was summoned and questioned by a teacher. I vehemently denied wishing him a happy Valentine's Day, which I had not. Instead, I had merely made an affirmative statement. That classmate would then go on to beat me up after school for merely telling him that. Every blow that rained down on me was accompanied by an insult. *Chhakka* (transvestite). *Baila* (pansy). *Gud* (faggot). The adage goes, 'Sticks and stones will break my bones, but words will never harm me.' Bullshit. I do not remember the pain of those blows. But those words still haunt me—every time I wear an outfit that is not conventional or giggle loudly or act slightly like a man is not supposed to (even though I am not a man), those words ring loud in my ears. And every time that happens, the shame comes back. Even now—when I am out and proud. I do police myself. I still remember the day after the NALSA judgment came out, a newspaper had carried pictures of trans people on the front page. It was waved in front of me. Those days are long gone but the shame that they gave me lives on. Every day I struggle with it, every day I fight it and grow more comfortable in my own skin.

I have happier memories of *Navtej*, though. I was going somewhere and I heard the announcement being made on the radio. I remember breaking down. I had not accepted even my own sexuality. Yet, I remember feeling like the weight of the world was no longer on my shoulders. A policeman could no longer threaten me with imprisonment.

But the story of *Naz*, NALSA, *Koushal* and *Navtej* are but flashpoints. I do not think that a movement as complex and diverse—if it can even be called a movement—can be spoken about through court cases only. What I do know, however, is that they tell us two things: One, that the court will not always be in our favour, and two, that we queers are a resilient bunch. We will fight, we will love, we will shock. Hell, we will even lose. But in the end, our enemies will fall. Section 377 fell. Non-recognition of queer marriages will fall. Review petitions have already been filed. We will come out stronger. Consider this: Utkarsh Saxena and Ananya Kotia went back to the Supreme Court the day after the judgment, when Utkarsh went down on one knee and proposed. In a moving post on X (formerly Twitter) Kotia wrote:

Yesterday hurt. Today, @utkarsh__saxena and I went back
to the court that denied our rights, and exchanged rings.
So this week wasn't about a legal loss, but our engagement.
We'll return to fight another day.

I think this speaks more of the resilience of queer people than
anything else.

Before I end this chapter, I do want to pay tribute to the
work done by the folks at Orinam and other collectives like
Orinam who do vital work in collecting and collating the
records of the cases and making them accessible publicly
much before the age of live-streaming and live-tweeting. It is
the work of organizations like Orinam and countless others
that the movement thrives.

Chapter 4

Acerbity, Acrimony and Arguments

Whenever the faggots leave their small liberated areas to enter the
spaces of the men, they cause scenes. They do not really mean to
do this. But the men cannot resist looking, pointing, yelling, or pushing
the faggots. Let two faggots kiss discreetly in the dark corner of a crowded
restaurant and pandemonium will break out. Let two faggots begin
to rub their bodies together rhythmically to some slow melody and
hissing will begin. The faggots have accepted all that they know and
see as the way things are and so can no longer be shocked. The men live
in the fantasy that everyone is like them and so are constantly shocked.
—Larry Mitchell, *Faggots and Their Friends*
between Revolutions[1]

After the Navtej judgment, Menaka Guruswamy and
Arundhati Katju in an Oxford Union address announced
'The Marriage Project', which was, in their opinion, the future
of LGBT rights in the world's largest democracy, a project
that would ensure marriage equality for queer couples. So,
in a way, the community knew that petitions would be filed
seeking marriage equality sooner rather than later.

It was in 2020, two years after *Navtej*, that the first
petition was filed by the Kerala High Court. Nikesh and

Sonu, a married gay couple from Thrissur, moved a plea before the Kerela High Court seeking to register their marriage under the SMA. The registration of marriage was refused by the district officer under the Act, stating that a homosexual marriage was not recognized under law. A single judge, Justice Anu Sivaraman, issued a notice on the matter.[2] Their petition made a powerful plea for marriage equality. It said that the decision of the Supreme Court in *Navtej* was 'meaningless and incomplete unless the sexual minorities are afforded equal access to the institution of marriage and by enabling them to profess love in the way they deem fit'.

Meanwhile, in the Delhi High Court, another petition titled Abhijit Iyer-Mitra v. Union of India, the petition sought recognition of marriage between, 'any two Hindus', based on a plain reading of Section 5 of the Hindu Marriage Act (HMA). There were also petitions filed under the SMA, the Foreign Marriage Act (FMA) and others which sought, broadly, the recognition of queer marriages. The Union of India challenged the maintainability of the petitions, stating that marriage between 'two individuals of the same gender was neither recognized nor accepted in any uncodified personal law or any codified statutory law'. The Union of India, in its affidavit before the Delhi High Court, said that a marriage could only be solemnized between a *biological* man, and a *biological* woman, and that living together was not in consonance with the Indian family unit. The affidavit noted, 'In our country, despite statutory recognition of the relationship of marriage between a biological man and a biological woman, marriage necessarily depends upon age-old customs, rituals, practices, cultural ethos and societal values.'

The proceedings in the Delhi High Court were rancorous, to say the least. The virulent pushback was evident even at the stage of pleadings. The Union of India chose to create hindrances for the smallest of issues as a way to derail the proceedings. The same tactic continued in the Supreme Court. Take, for example, an application which was filed for live-streaming of the proceedings before the Delhi High Court on the ground that this issue concerned citizens around the country. The Centre opposed even that. In the affidavit, the Ministry of Law and Justice said that the purpose of the applicant was to create a smokescreen of public interest and sensationalize the issue. Neeraj Kishan Kaul, the senior counsel who appeared on behalf of the petitioners, and the brother of Justice Sanjay Kishan Kaul, argued, 'I am troubled that the Government of India should use words like sympathy, hallucination, you are sensationalizing. You may agree or disagree on live-streaming but please don't trivialize and demean the people who have struggled for years till the Constitution bench of the apex court recognized their rights.'

This acrimony in some way has come to exemplify how affidavits are filed by the central government and how it conducts any case: Litigation has now become a stage for vehemently attacking the petitioners, their counsel and anyone that seeks any review of governmental action when it concerns the union government. The government sees any form of opposition as unpalatable and something that must be crushed. Thankfully, the division bench of Justice Vipin Sanghi and Navin Chawla came down heavily on the Union. 'Have you read the affidavit? We advise you not to have it on record and have a relook. This is not correct. As a counsel, it is your responsibility to read it and say that there is something objectionable. You are not obliged to follow it. You should be able to advise your client accordingly. Don't do a mindless exercise on this,' they said.[3]

Meanwhile, petitions were also filed in the Supreme Court seeking recognition of marriages under various laws in weeks of CJI Chandrachud taking over the office on the superannuation of his predecessor, Justice Uday Umesh Lalit. In November 2022, the Union of India made a statement at the hearing that the Ministry of Law and Justice was planning to transfer cases from around the country on marriage equality before the Supreme Court. Under Article 139A of the Constitution of India, the Supreme Court has the power to transfer cases—it can do so if it thinks that there is a question of law which is similar or substantially similar, and is pending before a different high court to itself.

After this, several more petitions were filed by people from across the country seeking recognition of marriage for queer couples. Two amongst them were petitions which I drafted and was a part of the legal team for, led by Anand Grover, a senior advocate.

The first petition was that of Sameer Samudra and his partner, Amit Gokhale, seeking recognition of marriage under the HMA. The second was that of Nitin Karani and Thomas Joseph, an interfaith couple seeking recognition of their marriage under the SMA.

Subsequently, on 6 January 2023, the Supreme Court transferred all matters from around the country to itself. On the date of these hearings, a group calling itself the United Hindu Front protested outside the Supreme Court. It claimed, 'These type of petitions are being filed time and again to destroy our ancient civilized traditions', ignoring the hard evidence on ancient culture in the stories of Ardhanarishwara or the temple depictions in Khajuraho. That is not to say queer people were accepted then, but they were present during ancient and medieval India.

Meanwhile, the government had filed an affidavit claiming that marriage equality or marriage between queer couples was an 'urban elitist' phenomenon—a claim that the court thumpingly rejected. The government averred that the Supreme Court should first decide whether it could legislate the 'separate socio-legal institution of marriage' between persons not contemplated for marriage rights under the existing law. This was quite an interesting framing of the argument. It had already declared that the Supreme Court would be legislating or creating a new law. In effect, the Supreme Court was called upon by those of us who were petitioners to interpret the existing law, something squarely within its domain. The Union had argued that marriage 'necessarily and inevitably' presupposes a union between two persons of the opposite sex.

Two months later, the matter was referred to a Constitution bench of five judges. Under Article 145, in any case involving a substantial question of law as to the interpretation of the Constitution, a minimum of five judges of the Supreme Court are required to hear the case. In this way, the Supreme Court is the final arbiter of any dispute concerning the Constitution and the final interpreter of the Constitution.

Common compilations of cases, legislation and documents, along with written submissions, were prepared by both sides. The record ran into tens of thousands of pages. Various states, including Gujarat and Madhya Pradesh, sought to intervene. There was a flurry of statements issued opposing marriage equality, from retired judges to the Bar Council of India, from religious groups to the National Commission for the Protection of Child Rights (NCPCR). One thing was clear: The fight was not going to be easy by any standards. The battle was an uphill one. We were asking the court to do what it had not done so far in the past few years: Go against the government on an issue that was seen to be a major concern. Remember, when *Navtej* was being argued, the

BJP-led central government had chosen not to take any stand. That is why, perhaps, Section 377 was read down. The NJAC, which would have allowed the government to appoint judges, was struck down perhaps out of a sense of self-preservation. As the old joke goes: 'Nothing irks a judge more than being told what he cannot do.' Be that as it may, we were eager and willing to go on.

* * *

18 April: Day One

The day dawned and the judges walked in. After the courtesy bow, Solicitor General Tushar Mehta got up. Before the petitioners could open their case, he said that the court could not venture into the creation of the socio-legal relation of marriage. He vehemently added that the court must, at the outset, resolve the preliminary objection of the Union of India, namely that the issue of regulation of marriage is the domain of competent legislature. Since the entry on marriage was in the concurrent list, and that the states were not joined, the petition was non-maintainable. He said that the government had to file an application, calling upon the court to decide first on the preliminary question. The Solicitor General's argument was this: The Supreme Court had issued a notice in January and the matter was not heard on its merits thereafter, on whether the court had the competence to hear the issue, and at the preliminary stage, the court ought to recognize the potential repercussions if the court becomes the forum for a debate on conferring sanctity and legal recognition to such marriages. The Chief Justice asked him to wait until the petitioners opened the case. He said that the arguments of the Union were a response to the petition on merits.

Mr Mehta then replied that preliminary objections were not objections on merits if merits were to be gone into. He said that he would limit his arguments and asked the petitioners to give an overview on their arguments. Sensing that the temperatures in the courtroom were rising and that the Solicitor General would not take no for an answer, the Chief Justice retorted, 'We're in charge, don't tell us how to conduct the proceedings.'

In an attempt to cajole the bench, Mr Mehta said that this was a sensitive issue and the court ought to look into the issue of an appropriate forum. But he wasn't done derailing the proceedings; he said he would have to take instructions on the issue. He said that this was not an issue on which the views of a farmer were known. These were arguments of alarm. A farmer, a doctor or for that matter anyone's views on issues of fundamental rights are irrelevant. What matters is whether the Constitution confers such a right, or whether such a right can be conferred on the citizen.

Mr Mukul Rohatgi, who was supposed to open the case for the petitioners, said this was not an issue of simple dismissal of a regular civil dispute. This was an issue of fundamental rights. Mr Mehta then said that none of these views represented the views of the nation. But the court is not a place for majoritarian ideas. A case does not have to represent the views of the nation. Any person seeking an enforcement of his rights and an adjudication on them is free to move the courts.

With this set of arguments, the ground was cleared for Mr Rohatgi to open the case. He made a passionate plea for why marriage equality ought to be recognized. He said that the people before the court were persons who are in same-sex relationships, who are said to have the same rights under

the Constitution as heterosexuals in society. This was a sexual
minority, he argued, and the only stumbling block to equality
was Section 377 by virtue of which sexual intercourse and sexual
acts were criminalized. So, he argued, queer couples could not
be equal to heterosexual couples. He then went on to talk
about how criminality was now gone and the 'unnatural' part
was erased from the statute. As a logical sequitur, he said if the
rights were identical, then the queer community must get to
enjoy all rights under Articles 14, 19 and 21 to lead a dignified
life to the fullest extent, which would include not just privacy
at home but also the right to express oneself without stigma in
public places. He said that the community desired the same
treatment insofar as the concept of marriage and family was
looked at in society.

In essence, he argued, the petitioners would seek a
declaration that they had a right to get married, that right would
be recognized by the State and marriage would be registered
under the SMA and other Acts. 'We have the rights, and the
State must recognize that right,' he roared. I remember being
in court at this moment. There were nods of affirmation from
queer people present in the courtroom. This was perhaps one
of the most powerful moments in the case.

At this point, the Chief Justice interjected and posed a
question, 'Assuming you seek a declaration from the court,
does that mean that same-sex couples have [the] right to
marry, and state should recognize—do you say SMA recognizes
the right already?'

Rohatgi had an answer ready. He argued that the provisions
of the SMA were made in 1954, and that society had evolved
since then. He said that the court may broadly read 'spouses'
as 'man' and 'woman'. A classic example of the definition of
marriage in Black's Dictionary originally said that marriage

was a union between a man and a woman. In the 2019 version, however, he said that the definition was changed to marriage as being a union of two persons. The argument was that the nature of marriage and how the law understood the institution of marriage had changed. He then took the court through the history of Indian law, on the Hindu Code bill, how women were accorded the right to property and an equal share in ancestral property. He argued that the Constitution is a living document, a document which must evolve with time. He said that the values in the Preamble, of equality, liberty and fraternity, ran through the Constitution: The petitioners before the court are citizens, and we were a part of 'all'—we must get our rights.

At this point, I guess, the judges had started to get into the contours of what the case was. The Chief Justice said that there were two parts to the issue: First, the declaration of the right to marriage as a fundamental right under Articles 14, 15 and 21; and if this were so, then it would necessitate recognition by interpretation of the SMA. He asked Rohatgi if we were touching religious personal laws.

Rohatgi replied in the affirmative that the petitioners were touching only the SMA and partly the HMA. He showed the bench how the definition clause starts with 'unless the context otherwise requires', showing that this represents the elasticity of legislation and demonstrates that as time passes, this would change. It was imperative to the courts that they could do it by interpretative tools. He took the question of whether the legislature ought to do it—Rohatgi said that the argument that the court must wait for the legislature to act arose in other cases too: *Navtej* on decriminalization, *Shayra Bano* on the constitutional validity of instant triple talaq for Muslims and also in *Puttuswamy* on the right to privacy. He said that the court need not wait for legislative interference, and if the court were to find in favour of the petitioners that there was a violation of fundamental rights, it was the court's duty to act.

The former Attorney General's next leg of argument was something I disagree with. He said, 'Our lives are passing by; we want respectability of a couple. What is the point of saying criminality in a room is removed, but in a public place, what about it?' He argued that the public perception of immorality or criminality was in itself an infringement of fundamental rights. He drew attention to various judgments of the court—on striking down bans on dancing in bars in *Anuj Garg*,[4] of discriminative employment conditions surrounding pregnancy for the air hostess in *Air India v. Nargesh Mishra*[5]—to show how the Supreme Court had extensively dealt with substantive equality and sex discrimination. Herein is my disagreement with this line of argument: What is a 'respectable couple'? Marriage is a legitimate legal need, but not a need for respectability. In her classic text *The Second Sex* Simone de Beauvoir[6] argues the fact that marriage automatically confers bourgeois respectability on its participants, and that seemed to be the argument that was advanced. I do not go that far. My argument is simple: There are instances in law that pragmatically require a recognition of marriage. Adoption of kids, making medical decisions and obtaining citizenship in some countries all require a valid and legally recognized marriage. But to argue that marriage is the sole way of attaining respectability, or that it is essential for respectability, was in my respectful submission a stretch. As Benoit Denizet-Lewis noted in his piece for the *New York Times*: 'Many young gay men don't see themselves as all that different from their heterosexual peers, and many profess to want what they've long seen espoused by mainstream American culture: a long-term relationship and the chance to start a family.'[7]

Rohatgi then went on to show the court how the court had, in *NALSA*, envisaged the constitutional right to equality for transgender persons. He said that the court had said that there must be two phases of the right to equality: A negative part, that is, a prohibition on discrimination, and second, a positive obligation on the State to ensure affirmative action by treating transgender persons as a socially and economically backward class of citizens for the purposes of reservation. He argued that no ministry had done anything with respect to reservations yet and the community was forced to move the court. Using this analogy, he said, the court had removed one layer of discrimination that was criminality. Now, it was time to bring the community into the public sphere. The community was a part of one homogenous whole, but within it were differences of caste, creed and religion. He then spoke about when a Constitution bench of nine judges had held that the items inserted into Schedule IX were subject to judicial review. The court also held secularism and equality were a part of the basic structure. If that were so, he said, how could we be denied the right to equality?

He then handed over a chart to the bench tracing the legal history of criminalization of a homosexual relationship and the recognition of marriage equality. He began with Lord Thomas Babington Macaulay who drafted the Indian Penal Code and introduced criminalization of homosexuality in Section 377, and how the Sexual Offences Act legalized homosexuality in England in 1967. From there he went to Lawrence v. Texas in the United States.[8] The issue was that there was a raid in Mr Lawrence's house, during which they found him indulging in homosexual activities in 1998. They were charged with misdemeanour under Texas law, which was ruled as unconstitutional by the Texas Court of Appeals. Finally, this was upheld by the United States Supreme Court in a 6–3 decision. On a side note, Justice Kennedy, who wrote the majority opinion, wrote in *Lawrence*,

> Moral disapproval of a group cannot be a legitimate governmental interest under the Equal Protection Clause because legal classifications must not be 'drawn for the purpose of disadvantaging the group burdened by the law'. Id., at 633. Texas' invocation of moral disapproval as a legitimate state interest proves nothing more than Texas' desire to criminalize homosexual sodomy. But the Equal Protection Clause prevents a State from creating 'a classification of persons undertaken for its own sake. Id., at 635.

And because Texas so rarely enforces its sodomy law as applied to private, consensual acts, the law serves more as a statement of dislike and disapproval against homosexuals than as a tool to stop criminal behaviour. The Texas sodomy law 'raise[s] the inevitable inference that the disadvantage imposed is born of animosity toward the class of persons affected'. This was the exact argument that those of us representing the petitioners were making. Legal classification that the State was choosing to make cannot be sustained on the touchstone of constitutional principles, that is, the State cannot treat equals unequally for disadvantaging a group.

Rohatgi then went on to rip the affidavit of the Union to shreds: He showed how the counter-affidavit of the Union relied on a 1967 definition of Black's Law Dictionary. The 2019 Act, which spoke of marriage as a union between two persons, was the definition which Black's Law Dictionary adopted after looking at how society has evolved. He then spoke of the two petitioners in the first case he represented: A gay couple—two individuals who loved each other and wanted to reach the status of a married couple; they wanted a family. He argued that the

Supreme Court had, in *Navtej*, held that queer persons cannot be sent to jail, and now, as a logical next step, their marriage must be recognized to ensure inclusion in society.

Rohatgi then argued that if there was a fundamental right under Articles 14 or 19 to be treated as equals, then the full enjoyment of the right to be equal must necessarily include the right to a dignified life, which includes the right to choose a partner for marriage. He argued that the recognition should be the same as that offered to others. He asserted that the lives of queer persons were passing by, and that they cannot wait for their rights to be recognized. He argued that the Supreme Court itself had recognized the right to equality and equal rights in various decisions, and now the time had come for the Supreme Court to enforce the rights. He argued that only if the State recognized equality would society and then workplaces and other places recognize that queer persons are equal and they should stop discriminating.

He then went on to speak about the role that the Supreme Court played in our body politic. He said if there were fundamental rights involved, the doors of the Supreme Court had to be thrown open to citizens. He argued that discrimination was happening in real life, but at the same time, queer relationships were being accepted slowly because no longer criminal, but this process could be catalysed by recognizing the right to marriage. He spoke of how the judgments of the Supreme Court were binding on all courts of law under Article 141. If this were true, and that such a right existed, what role should the court play in recognizing and enforcing that right, he asked. He said that the courts do this through the process of interpretation of fundamental rights and then leave it to Parliament to formalize it in law by amending a law or by introducing a new law. He argued that the law was not static but evolving. When called upon, it was the duty of the court to act.

At this point, the Chief Justice intervened, asking again how the court should go about deciding the matter. He said that if the court were to rule in our favour, and declare that the right to marry was a fundamental right, then the court had two options: First, it could either find a legislative void as Parliament does not recognize the right to marry and then ask them to amend accordingly; or second, locate modalities for implementing the right by bringing in a new Act. It was an expected question, and Rohatgi hit it out of the park. He argued that in *Vishaka*, where the court was faced with the issue of sexual harassment at the workplace, the Supreme Court laid down an interim law in the form of a set of guidelines framed by the court which was to be the law till Parliament acted. Those guidelines later found a place in the Sexual Harassment of Women at Workplace (Prevention, Prohibition and Redressal) Act, 2013. Here, according to him, there was a past history of Parliament enacting a law on marriage in the form of various personal laws and the SMA, as opposed to sexual harassment where prior to 2013 there wasn't any history. So it was argued that all the court has to do is interpret the statute creatively and in favour of the queer community.

At this point, multiple counsels got up to address the court on that issue. Mr K.V. Viswanathan, who went on to be elevated to the bench of the Supreme Court a few days after the case had been argued, the judgement had been reserved that confining marriage to heterosexual couples was constitutionally impermissible. He argued that other people, that is, heterosexual and cisgender people, have fundamental rights recognized otherwise. He argued that Parliament has to tailor laws to bring them in accordance with fundamental rights. Viswanathan argued that the court could not wait for them and submit to popular will, which was anathema to the very notion of fundamental rights. Dr Menaka Guruswamy raised important concerns about the HMA. She said that the HMA is an issue of statutory law and not personal law, and that reforms are always said in the context of personal law. The court has to aim at making statutory law workable. The Chief Justice also raised issues about other personal laws and said that the court had to be mindful that by the process of interpretation, there was some element of judicial discretion. There was no denial of the legislative element involved. He said, 'We don't have to decide anything to decide something.'

Justice Kaul chipped in then. He said that the court had to construe the SMA in incremental changes since there were issues of social and society-wide ramifications. There was a time for everything to come. He asked whether the SMA could be interpreted to read into it a gender-neutral understanding. At this point, for the first time, the Chief Justice asked a question which made me realize that the bench was perhaps not with us. He went on to ask how the court could develop the notion of a civil union which finds recognition in a statute. Note this. The terms of the debate had suddenly shifted to civil unions when none of the petitions asked for it. Certain petitions on the other hand, such as Rituparna Borah's petition were completely different and argued for 'chosen families' and protection from natal family violence, which meant that there was complete freedom to allow individuals to allocate familial rights to individuals that they chose.

Guruswamy proposed that the issue before the court was not merely of marriage but the bouquet of rights that queer persons were denied access to, such as insurance (life, medical) and bank accounts. Adding a personal touch to her arguments, she pointed out how she could not buy the medical insurance that the Supreme Court Bar Association provides for its members. She said that the rights were essential to protect relationships, and the question before the court was that of the day-to-day business of life. She pointed out how the law in India says rights flow from blood relations, marriage or adoption. Anything short of full marriage, she argued, would make sure that individual issues of discrimination keep coming to court.

At this point, Justice Kaul said that the court could not potentially answer all questions of discrimination. It was now becoming clear to a lot of us that the bench thought that perhaps the issue was too wide for it to make a decision on. Dr Abhishek Manu Singhvi said that if the bench wanted to it could limit it to the SMA, but there were two crucial aspects: Marriage and the persons that the court would have to consider. He argued that this was not a same-sex marriage, but a 'same-person marriage' (sic). The idea, I imagine, is that he wanted to focus on personhood. He argued that if marriage was recognized but there were no consequential benefits, then the declaration by the court would be an empty shell. He argued that there were two sets of differences: sex-based and gender-based. Most petitions, he argued, were not arguing personal laws, and that could perhaps be left for another day. The inaccurate description of marriage notwithstanding, this intervention by Dr Singhvi brought a good understanding of gender as a spectrum before the court.

At this point Justice Kaul wondered if the court could decide not to touch personal law and read 'person' instead of the phrase 'man and woman' under the SMA, leaving everything else for the future. Notice how the canvas was always shifting for the petitioners.

The Solicitor General got up and said that there was no law governing rights and immunities for the queer community save for *NALSA* and *Navtej*. He argued that the Transgender Act, in 2019, covered most aspects, but consciously left out marriage. He read out various definitions from the Act including 'establishment', 'family', 'inclusive education', 'institution' and 'transgender person' under Section 2(k). He argued that the Act protects any sexual offences and provides for discrimination to be criminally prosecuted. He further argued that there were statutory obligations on governments to take steps to secure inclusion and participation. He said that there were windows which were already opened; now the community wanted to open doors. He argued that the societal acceptance of a relationship was never dependent on legislation or on judgments. Societal relations, the Solicitor General argued, come from within. 'All relations have been between a biological man and a biological woman'. This was a strange arc—the idea here was not just marriage but broader rights for the broader community. What followed was a heated exchange between the Solicitor General and the Chief Justice.

Chief Justice: The notion of biological man/woman is absolute, and that it cannot be changed, this is incorrect. There is no absolute concept of a man or woman. It cannot be a question of what your genitals are, it is far more complex.

Solicitor General: (*shouting*) Biological man means biological man . . . the genitals you have. For man, there are age limits prescribed. With this notion of non-absoluteness, [under Section] 160 CrPC, can a woman/man be confused—without taking into consideration the genitals? Parliamentary committees should deal with this . . . they are not acting like the Parliament, they have members from all parties—call witnesses, experts and stakeholders. Now [a] window of marriage was opened by *Navtej Singh*, now that window is leading to another

window—eventually the window of personal law will have to
be opened. Entry 5 of concurrent list—law of marriage, NOT
of personal law. Therefore, preliminary objection.

At this point, Mr Kapil Sibal, appearing for Jamiat Ulema-
e-Hind, jumped on the bandwagon, 'Who gets maintenance
post-divorce? Who is the father and mother under CrPC?
Don't do it piecemeal; it will create more problems for
that union. Other legislatures reform other laws with this.
Personally, I am all for it—either you do everything, or you
do nothing.'

Following this exchange, the Chief Justice was mercilessly
and viciously trolled. A report by Newslaundry[9] analysed
7,53,848 tweets of which 1,16,669 were original posts; of these,
268 tweets were copy-pasted around five times. The report
added that #notmycji was used 1747 times, #nosamesexmarriage
433   times,   #undemocraticsupremecourt   366   times,
#genderbiasedlaws 349 times and #judiciarymustapologise
256 times within the stipulated time.[10] Evidently, this is
organized trolling. Notably, his judgment in *Navtej* had made
similar observations, but that did not attract much attention.

Rakesh Dwivedi, appearing for the State of Madhya Pradesh,
argued that there was no equality between heterosexual and
homosexual couples. He stated that although the Supreme
Court had decriminalized homosexuality in *Navtej*, it was not
a ground for complete equality. To say I was seething at this
would be an understatement. In a manner of speaking, these
hearings were a test of patience. To have your lives subject to
petty, homophobic debate masked as legal arguments, to be
told that you are not an equal, riles you up like nothing else
can. And when these submissions are made before the highest
constitutional court, with no censure from the bench, it is

even worse. I am not saying that the other side should not be heard. They should be and they must be. But the level of legal discourse during these proceedings was shallow. It was the same courtroom where Justice Khanna said that Nani Palkhivala spoke as if divinity was speaking through him. Surely, we must, as lawyers appearing before such courts, maintain a level of legal discourse befitting the stature of the Supreme Court.

Rohatgi began his arguments again. He exclaimed that he was amazed to hear that queer people were not equal to the heterosexual group. He said that the Constitution makes only one class: 'We, the people of India'. Merely removing the obstacle of Section 377 still allowed discrimination to be rampant in society. The state was bound to create equality. All people became equal in 1950, and that value was created through the Preamble to the Constitution. *Kesavananda Bharati*[11] and *Puttuswamy*[12] also re-emphasized the value of equality being central to our constitutional scheme.

He then went back to talking about the whole phrasing by the Union of India of queerness being an urban elite phenomenon. He dealt with it through history and mythology. First, he spoke about the Roman emperor Nero who married two men in 1858 and told the imperial court to recognize that marriage. Second, he told the court of the birth of Lord Ayyappa who was born out of the union of Lord Shiva and Lord Vishnu (in the form of Mohini) in Indian mythology. He argued that how society looks at issues and concepts changes. Drawing on the example of widow remarriage, he argued that society did not recognize their right, but the courts did. Similarly, after *Navtej*, there was a perceptible shift in society's perception towards queerness. Similarly, here, the court had the powers to shift the views of society, he said.

Mere disdain from the majority cannot preclude constitutional rights, Rohatgi proclaimed. The core of his argument was that the exercise of rights cannot be according to majoritarian will, and thus Parliament cannot be left to decide. Borrowing from *Koushal*, Rohatgi argued that the queer community was called a minuscule minority, faced discrimination, was sidetracked, and that there was a feeling amongst members of the community that they were 'unpopular', and the 'queer' word itself was subjected to stigmatization. The court was in a position to do something about it, and he argued that discrimination is deeply offensive to an individual's self-esteem and dignity and placed on equal footing. He said, 'Let us not model ourselves on Nero'—I assume he meant it in the context of Nero playing a fiddle while Rome burnt and not on him seeking recognition of his marriage to two men. Rohatgi said that sexuality and gender were not elitist concepts, but an innate choice.

The Chief Justice said that there were two corresponding rights and duties: On the one hand, the queer community is entitled to say that it has the right to make its own choices and live together as it wishes, and that is a part of our dignity and privacy. But equally, he said that society cannot say, 'All right, we recognize that right and we leave you alone; we will not recognize your relationship.' He said it was not enough to leave queer people alone, but to assert the right to have the recognition of these social institutions. Rohatgi agreed, and went back to Goethe's dictum that Justice Misra had relied on in *Navtej*, 'I am what I am, therefore take me as I am.' He argued that the doctrine of transformative constitutionalism necessitated that constitutional and statutory interpretation move on with the times. He said that the law could be laid down either by the court under Article 141 or by Parliament.

With this, the first day of arguments ended. Rohatgi framed marriage as one of the requirements Indian society and parents have for queer persons to 'settle down', as an institution which allowed respectability. There were plenty of fireworks: From the Solicitor General threatening to not appear in the proceedings, to watching him shout out 'biological man is man' in the face of the Chief Justice, and thus pointing out that 'biological man' is not a contingent notion. He argued that men and women can recognized by their genitals, ignoring the judgement in *NALSA*.

I think it was here that I first figured out that this case was not going to be easy. It became evident that the lawyer, the queer and the activist in me were going to be in conflict. As a junior lawyer, one is supposed to be seen and not heard, and be useful to the senior that one is briefing. But when such mockery was made of life, how could one be quiet? My journal entry from that day has only three words: 'conflict, exhaustion, rage'.

* * *

19 April: Day Two

The second day started with yet another stonewalling attempt by the Union of India to derail the hearings. The Solicitor General, Tushar Mehta, again raised the issue of states not being parties to the hearings in court. He informed the court that the Union of India had written to all the chief secretaries of the states. The Chief Justice saw right through it and retorted, 'That's excellent. So that now it's not that the States are unaware. You have informed them that [if] somebody has to say something they will come.' The Solicitor General reiterated his argument that notice ought to be served to the states. At this juncture, I think it becomes important to point one thing out. The matter was widely publicized, and so, if the states wanted to intervene in the case, they could have been heard like the numerous other intervenors were. They chose not to be involved. So issuing a notice would have done little but delay the proceedings.

Mukul Rohatgi resumed his argument that the challenge was made to a central law, and thus, the opposition party which was necessary was the Union of India. Merely because a matter lay in the concurrent list, there was no rationale for saying non-joinder of states should lead to a dismissal of the petition. Under our Constitution, the list on which the Union and the states can legislate is found in Schedule VIII, read with Article 246 of the Constitution. There are three lists. List I consists of matters on which only the Union, that is, Parliament, can legislate. This includes matters like foreign policy, defence, etc. List II has matters on which only the states can legislate such as prisons, police, public health, etc. List III has matters on which both the Union and the states can legislate. Entry 5 of List III reads as follows: 'Marriage and divorce; infants and minors; adoption; wills, intestacy and succession; joint family and partition; all matters in respect of which parties in judicial proceedings were immediately before the commencement of this Constitution subject to their personal law.' There are, of course, exceptions to this rule, but going into that is not required for the purposes of this litigation.

Rohatgi then pointed out that notices were issued to other respondents in the matter over five months ago. There was an undue delay when the letter was written only on the previous day. He pointed out that the issue of insolvency was also in the concurrent list, and when the provisions of the insolvency and bankruptcy code were challenged, the states were not made parties. The Chief Justice once again reiterated that they would still listen to the states should they wish to intervene.

Rohatgi then continued his arguments from the previous day. He argued that emanating from the inalienable right to privacy, the right to sexual privacy must be granted. He said that it should have the sanctity of a natural right and be protected under the Constitution as fundamental to liberty, and as a soulmate of dignity. He used this to argue that there must be a declaration from the court that there is a fundamental right to be married which can be worn as a badge of honour by members of the queer community. He argued that there was no touching of personal laws, but the secular law must move forward. Demonstrating to the court the importance of marriage, he demonstrated how gratuity and pension are provided only to those spouses who have survived the death of their retired partners. Another example that was cited was that a gift under the Income Tax Act to a spouse is non-taxable. He showed various other examples, including clauses under the Motor Vehicles Act, the Juvenile Justice Act, etc. Justice Bhat then pointed out that this would also include personal laws, and so even though the canvas was already limited by the court to secular law, the court would have to engage with secular law. So, he said, that even though the matter may be truncated here, it was an organic whole.

Rohatgi's next argument was that the SMA should be made gender-neutral by a declaration that 'person' ought to be read wherever 'man and woman' is used. The argument was that in the SMA, the words 'husband' and 'wife' should be used as 'spouse', and 'man and woman' as 'person'. A large part of this would solve the projected interpretation of the SMA. He said it was important to destroy the heteronormative framework of marriage. At this point, Justice Kaul intervened and said one fine day things cannot be changed, and they evolve gradually.

Rohatgi then took the court through four judgments: *Shakti Vahini*,[13] *Shafin Jahan*,[14] *Laxmibai Chandaragi*[15] and *Deepika*,[16] four judgments which lay down that every person is entitled to marry a person of his/her own choice, and were either inter-caste or inter-religious marriages. The argument was that if heterosexual couples are entitled to marry persons of their choice, and if heterosexual couples and queer couples are equal, then queer couples ought to have the same right to marry a person of their choice.

The next argument was on the right to privacy. He argued that intimacies of a marriage lie within a core zone of privacy, which is inviolable. Such a right would mean that the right of a person to choose a life partner is not dependent on societal approval. Consider widow remarriage, where the law acted with alacrity. Based on this, Rohatgi argued that it was the job of the court and the law to push society. He said that they had done so by annulling Section 377, but it had to now move ahead with a declaration that members of the queer community can marry.

He spoke about the regression of the law in the United States in *Dobbs*[17] and the overruling of Roe v. Wade.[18] There have been times when the court has failed. All discordant notes, the former Attorney General said, have been corrected by this court: *ADM Jabalpur*, *M.P. Sharma* and many others. The Supreme Court is the guarantor and protector of fundamental rights. If India has to go forward, then the Supreme Court must take the lead with its moral and legal authority to show society the norm and ask it to remove dogma and stigma. He further argued that the power, jurisdiction, obligation and responsibility which was cast on the Supreme Court under the Constitution is only cast on this court, not even the high courts. This was the role of the final protector of rights and the arbiter of what the law is and what the rights are. If the State accepts a majoritarian view of morality as being correct, the citizenry is left with little option yet it retains the power and the right to come to this court. Rohatgi then pointed out how the queer community has no voice in Parliament, and the only redressal left to it as citizens is to plead before the court. He argued that the court would fail in its duty if it failed to protect the rights of the common citizen. He said that the idea of the State adhering to constitutional morality must become a habit, and it could only become so when the Supreme Court laid down the law.

On a side note, when Alexander Hamilton wrote *The Federalist Papers*[19] in the United States, he called the judiciary 'the least powerful branch'. This, he said, was because neither did it have control over the purse strings as it was controlled by the legislature, nor could it exercise the might of the sword like the executive. What the courts had was only their moral authority. However, unlike the United States, India's Supreme Court has the power to punish for contempt and compel the execution of its orders. Under Article 144 of the Constitution, all authorities, whether they are civil or judicial, are duty-bound to act in aid of the Supreme Court. No head of State can act like Andrew Jackson, who had refused to enforce the decision of the US Supreme Court in Worcestor v. Georgia, which was authored by Justice John Marshall and had defiantly proclaimed:[20] 'John Marshall has made his decision; now let him enforce it!'

The next issue that came up was the gender-neutral interpretation of the SMA. Justice Hima Kohli asked if 'any person' has to be read in place of man/woman in Schedule I, then Part 1 and 2 of the Schedule of the SMA coalesce. Schedule I has two parts which talk about prohibited degrees of marriage: Part 1 talks about female relatives while Part 2 talks about male relatives. Marriage with relatives that fall within the first or second parts is prohibited under Section 4(d) of the SMA.

Rohatgi then took the bench through Section 4 of the SMA. For the purposes of convenience, I will reproduce the section below. Section 4 reads as follows:

> 4. **Conditions relating to solemnization of special marriages**—Notwithstanding anything contained in any other law for the time being in force relating to the solemnization of marriages, a marriage between any two persons may be solemnized under this Act, if at the time of the marriage the following conditions are fulfilled, namely:
>
> a. Neither party has a spouse living;
> b. Neither party—
>   i. Is incapable of giving a valid consent to it in consequence of unsoundness of mind; or
>   ii. Though capable of giving a valid consent, has been suffering from mental disorder of such a kind or to such an extent as to be unfit for marriage and the procreation of children; or
>   iii. Has been subject to recurrent attacks of insanity
> c. The male has completed the age of twenty-one years and the female the age of eighteen years;
> d. The parties are not within the degrees of prohibited relationship.
>
> Provided that where a custom governing at least one of the parties permits of a marriage between them, such marriage may be solemnized, notwithstanding that they are within the degrees of prohibited relationship; and:

e. Where the marriage is solemnized in the state of Jammu and Kashmir, both parties are citizens of India domiciled in the territories to which this Act extends.

Explanation.—In this section, 'custom', in relation to a person belonging to any tribe, community, group or family means any rule which the state government may, by notification in the Official Gazette, specify in this behalf as applicable to members of that tribe, community, group or family:

Provided that no such notification shall be issued in relation to the members of any tribe, community, group or family, unless the state government is satisfied—

i. That such rule has been continuously and uniformly observed for a long time among those members;
ii. That such rule is certain and not unreasonable or opposed to public policy; and
iii. That such rule, if applicable only to a family, has not been discontinued by the family.

He showed the bench how in Section 4(a), the word used was 'person', and in 4(b), the word used was 'spouse'; in 4(c), which talks about the age of marriage, the section had used 'males' and 'females' which was to be left as is. Justice Bhat then posed a question that the idea of this litigation was to move beyond male and female. What happens to transgender persons? He said that the issue was that the court could not even neglect heterosexual couples and the protections which were given to their vulnerabilities in respect of child marriages.

The Chief Justice then wondered that if there was a gay couple then the statute could be read harmoniously as the age being twenty-one, and for a lesbian couple, the age could be read as eighteen. The issue arose for transgender people, and the Chief Justice asked if the court could read it as twenty-one for all purposes. Rohatgi acquiesced. Justice Bhat again spoke about other people on the gender spectrum, and how they would get accommodated in such a reading. He said that such a reading of the SMA would entail going back to the social stereotype which the petitioners sought to dismantle. He said that this was a selective reading, and that while interpreting, the court had to look at all circumstances.

Rohatgi then took the court through other sections. I will reproduce the arguments first and then the section for convenience. He argued that for Sections 12 and 23, the words 'husband' and 'wife' ought to be read as 'spouse'.

The sections read as follows:

12. Place and form of solemnization.—(1) The marriage may be solemnized at the office of the marriage officer, or at such other place within a reasonable distance therefrom as the parties may desire, and upon such conditions and the payment of such additional fees as may be prescribed.

(2) The marriage may be solemnized in any form which the parties may choose to adopt:

Provided that it shall not be complete and binding on the parties unless each party says to the other in the presence of the marriage officer and the three witnesses and in any language understood by the parties,—'I, (A), take the (B), to be my lawful wife (or husband)'.

23. Judicial separation.—(1) A petition for judicial separation may be presented to the district court either by the husband or the wife:

    a.   On any of the grounds specified 3[in sub-section (1) 4[and sub-section (1A)] of Section 27] on which a petition for divorce might have been presented; or

    b.   On the ground of failure to comply with a decree for restitution of conjugal rights:

And the court, on being satisfied of the truth of the statements made in such petition, and that there is no legal ground why the application should not be granted, may decree judicial separation accordingly.

(2) Where the court grants a decree for judicial separation, it shall be no longer obligatory for the petitioner to cohabit with the respondent, but the court may, on the application by petition of either party and on being satisfied of the truth of the statements made in such petition, rescind the decree if it considers it just and reasonable to do so.

With this, Mukul Rohatgi finished his arguments. It fell now on Dr Abhishek Manu Singhvi to carry the baton. Singhvi, who represented Utkarsh Saxena and Ananya Kotia, is a senior advocate and a politician belonging to the Indian National Congress. Unlike Rohatgi whose style of argument in the case was a passionate plea, Dr Singhvi's arguments were clinical, but he brought with him his characteristic forensic brilliance that I have admired since I first saw him argue.

At the outset, Singhvi told the judges that they may not get answers to the questions that were posed in the same sequence that they were posed, but they would get the answers. He said that the matter was not about how to read the provisions of the statutes, but at its heart, the case was about choosing the most enduring relationship: The marital relationship. He argued that regardless of sex and sexual orientation, gender or gender identity, and to manifest the idea of love in marriage regardless of those factors, was a fundamental right. The obverse heart of this case was the discriminatory denial to a section of the community to do it based on these factors—this is the exclusion or discrimination which the petitioners were challenging. He then went on to speak about the role of *Navtej*: *Navtej*, he argued, was momentous for the removal of discrimination; it was essentially undoing prejudices. But little had been done since then. So now the court had to remove the next brick of discrimination.

He said his argument was going to be under three heads: First, the interpretation of the SMA in a Constitution-compliant manner on the touchstone of larger constitutional values enshrined in the Preamble and Part 2; second, asking for a declaration that the notice and objection regime was unconstitutional; and finally, the reliefs that the petitioners sought. He argued that for queer couples, it was not the State alone which imperilled the values of liberty, equality and fraternity. The values were also threatened by private groups (non-State actors) which were entrenched and entrusted forces with an invasive thought process to constitutional values. This court has to protect the vulnerable section from State and non-State actors. Justice Bhat said that these groups will continue to act as they do unless you say the State has to protect you from these actions. The State is bound to protect; even in free speech, the State plays a role. He asked what prevented the State from protecting queer couples. To this, Singhvi replied that these couples could not seek any rights as a result of their marriage not being recognized.

On a side note: Bhat's question demonstrated a complete lack of understanding of how queer couples interact with the State. Notably, it is the State which becomes an enabler and also a proponent of violence against queer couples. This evidence was produced by the petitioners in *NALSA* and the judgement takes cognizance of it. As Justice Radhakrishnan notes,

> Non-recognition of the identity of Hijras/transgender persons denies them equal protection of law, thereby leaving them extremely vulnerable to harassment, violence and sexual assault in public spaces, at home and in jail, also by the police. Sexual assault, including molestation, rape, forced anal and oral sex, gang rape and stripping is being committed with impunity and there are reliable statistics and materials to support such activities. Further, non- recognition of identity of Hijras /transgender persons results in them facing extreme discrimination in all spheres of society, especially in the field of employment, education, healthcare etc.

Singhvi then talked to the court about how a current prohibition on marriage for queer couples failed in the face of larger constitutional facets of non-discrimination, dignity and free speech. He argued that just like English courts can read a statute to make them compliant with European treaties, Indian courts have to read statutes to make them compliant with the Constitution.

He argued that sexual orientation and gender identity were ascriptive issues which were not bestowed upon an individual not by choice, largely involuntary such as caste and race. Here, he said it was sexual orientation and gender. Any implied exclusion of the entire LGBTQ class from the SMA is based on sole markers of identity: Sex and sexual orientation.

He then went on to the stand of the government which, in his opinion, was that marriage is a vital institution and the State must protect it. It lies at the heart of society, and the court is attacking society. He said that there were two kinds of marriages: Traditional and non-traditional marriages. In either case, for those who seek marriage, they seek it for the social validation of a relationship. He said that he could not agree more with the Solicitor General—just like heterosexuals seek and deserve it, non-heterosexuals also seek and deserve it. Marriage has consequences in the form of derivative rights and it is a gateway to those consequences.

At this point, the Chief Justice intervened and said that if a lesbian couple wants, one partner can easily adopt a child. If the court has decriminalized homosexuality, they are allowed to live together and one of them can adopt. It is just that the child would lose the benefit of parenthood. To which Singhvi then said that marital status by itself was a source of dignity, fulfilment and self-respect. It was thus a vital institution. He then took the court through various rights which accrued on marriage: Adoption, surrogacy, intestate succession, tax exemption, tax deduction, privilege (spousal communication), right to bodily remains, group insurance, etc.

At this point, Justice Bhat said that some things could be segregated and be given to queer people, provided that there is no such prohibition in the Parent Act.[21] Dr Menaka Guruswamy said that often there is no specific guideline on who has what rights. For example, she argued that the assumption is that if you are spouses, you can have a joint bank account. The moment the Supreme Court opened up the definition of marriage, these issues would be resolved automatically, she said. Dr Singhvi continued and said that marriage was the baseline.

He then attacked the idea of marriage equality being an 'urban elite' phenomenon. To this, the Chief Justice seemed to be in agreement and said that there was no data from the government to show that this was urban or rural; none at all. Mr K.V. Viswanathan (as he then was) then spoke of his client, Zainab Patel, who was forced to take to the streets, disowned by her family and reduced to begging. From there she rose to become a member of the National Council for Transgender Persons. He said that this demonstrated an absolute lack of grace from the Union. Ms Jayna Kothari, a senior advocate representing the transgender rights activist Akkai Padmashali, also spoke of her client, who at fifteen was thrown out of her house; she dropped out of school and then came out on her own. She said that the idea of marriage is cherished by the petitioners who are working-class people, to say this is an urban elite population is so wrong. Ms Karuna Nundy spoke of how hijras are not the urban elite.

The Chief Justice then said that the SMA was intended to be agnostic to faith. By reading it as agnostic to sexual orientation, the petitioners were not taking a leap of faith. Dr Singhvi agreed. He argued that societal values could not trump fundamental rights.

The next issue that Dr Singhvi addressed was the process of marriage equality in England. He argued that England was considered to be very timid in cases where judicial interpretation was required. He quoted a case and said, 'It is wrong to think that the text of some statute is a limitation, or that the intent is a limitation.' He argued that with the evolving dynamics of time and society, there were two tests which were employed in England to make statutes treaty-compliant, which in the Indian scenario must be read to mean

Constitution-compliant. These tests were (A) The underlying thrust of the legislation, and (B) The institutional capacity of the court, which means that the court was being asked to strip the legislation of its intent. Barring these, he said, nothing was a limitation on judicial review since the thrust and intent evolve with time. He said that in this case, the court did not have to strike down anything, but had to merely make it Constitution-compliant. He then read Justice Chandrachud's opinion in *Deepika Singh*[22] where the Supreme Court had held that atypical families also deserve the protection of the law.

Finally, he read the judgment of the House of Lords in Ghaidan v. Godin-Mendoza,[23] where the defendant and his gay partner were residing in a tenancy property. On the death of the partner, the landlord demanded possession since the tenancy was in favour of the deceased partner. While upholding the right of same-sex partners, the House of Lords held that while interpreting a statute, the courts can construe statutes disagreeing with their unambiguous meaning, ignoring the precise wording. However, the only limitation was that such an interpretation should not depart from the underlying thrust of the statute. The words of the House of Lords written by Baroness Hale of Richmond on equal treatment and democracy are quite moving. Let me reproduce a passage:

> Such a guarantee of equal treatment is also essential to democracy. Democracy is founded on the principle that each individual has equal value. Treating some as automatically having less value than others not only causes pain and distress to that person but also violates his or her dignity as a human being. The essence of the Convention, as has often been said, is respect for human

dignity and human freedom: see Pretty v. United Kingdom
(2002) 35 EHRR 1, 37, para 65. Second, such treatment
is damaging to society as a whole. Wrongly to assume that
some people have talent and others do not is a huge waste
of human resources. It also damages social cohesion,
creating not only an under-class, but an under-class with
a rational grievance. Third, it is the reverse of the rational
behaviour we now expect of government and the state.
Power must not be exercised arbitrarily. If distinctions
are to be drawn, particularly upon a group basis, it is
an important discipline to look for a rational basis for
those distinctions. Finally, *it is a purpose of all human rights
instruments to secure the protection of the essential rights of
members of minority groups, even when they are unpopular with
the majority. Democracy values everyone equally even if the
majority does not.*' (emphasis added)

With that, the second day's arguments ended. I want to draw
an important point here: At the beginning, Justice Kaul pointed
out the way all petitions asked for a different remedy. This is
characteristic of the queer movement in India—we are not talking
to each other. There is distrust, and hence a need for increased
conversation. More on that later. One of the arguments which
was made during the day was that if homosexuality is innate only
then is it respectable. But, if we choose it, it is elitist. This was
not called for by someone who was supposed to be representing
the community in court. This innateness, or ascriptive character
of queerness, ought to be an argument which should have
been avoided. There is no evidence which conclusively tells us
why we are queer. Even if it did, grounding queer politics in
respectability is dangerous for multiple reasons. Should bisexual
and pansexual people then be forced to confirm? This argument

of queerness being innate is an appeal to tolerance and mercy of society and not an argument in acceptance. Even the Chief Justice caught on to this.

The critique may be harsh and is not meant to disrespect any lawyer. It is made much after the arguments are over and the judgment is delivered. But a critical analysis of any battle, whether it is won or lost, is crucial in devising future strategy, and it is for this sole reason that I do that.

* * *

20 April: Day Three

The third day began with lawyers jostling with each other and the bench for time to address the court. Who gets to address the court and when is not just a matter of seniority, but also legal strategy.

Dr Singhvi continued his arguments on *Ghaidan* from the previous day. He argued that it was discriminatory to treat individuals differently based on their sexual orientation. He argued that the ability to achieve a convention-compliant result is not bound by the text of the statute. He argued that the court needed to look into the underlying intention or the thrust of the SMA. If that does not preclude or exclude marriage between a queer couple, then the text cannot bind the statute.

The Chief Justice intervened and said that for the SMA, the purpose was to provide a method or avenue for marriage beyond the religious methods which are recognized by law, and to address the issue of caste endogamy. He recognized correctly that the 1954 law was to allow for marriages which did not have social sanction.

It was Bhat's turn to intervene now. He said that the statute provided a framework for the concept of marriage which transcended the old ideas, and what the petitioners were saying amounted to the SMA providing a constitutional framework for marriage. Dr Singhvi replied that the institute departed from the existing sense of marriage already. He wondered whether the framework was cast in stone or it was evolving. Could the legislation withstand this thrust? The Chief Justice wondered if the court could straddle the line which divided policy from judicial process. He said that the impact of *Ghaidan* in the UK was to liberate the court from the traditional purpose. In India, socially and constitutionally, the courts have reached the intermediate state, according to the Chief Justice, who postulated that by decriminalizing homosexuality, the Act contemplates that people who belong to the same sex have been in marriage-like relationships. He further said that the moment the court says, 'homosexuality is no longer an offence, it contemplates a stable marriage-like relationship, and not [a] by-chance relationship. We contemplate stable emotional relationships. Once we have crossed that bridge, the next question is that can a statute recognize marriage-like relationships?' Dr Singhvi said it was little done, vast undone. The decriminalization of homosexuality was the first amongst many things. To which Justice Chandrachud replied that the court would have to redefine the concept of marriage. He said that two people of opposite sexes were a necessary requirement for marriage. He wondered if the law had progressed enough to say that people of the same sex could be married—that was the main question. He distinguished that unlike the United Kingdom, in India, there had always been overarching principles, and the strict separation of powers was absent. Singhvi replied that the case was only cited for interpretation purposes. At this point, the Chief Justice told Dr Singhvi that a relation between a man and a woman was so fundamental that if the Court considered a relation between a man and a man, it would mean redoing the entire tapestry of the statute. He also quipped that the institution of marriage was so important that denying it to same-sex couples would be contrary to fundamental rights.

Dr Singhvi then went on to show how in standard personal insurance, the term 'legally wedded spouse' is used by the Insurance Regulatory and Development Authority of India (IRDAI). If the court held that the SMA includes man and woman, they would be legally wedded spouses, he said. He argued that Section 2(b) in Schedule I of the Act would continue to apply both parts of the Schedule will have to apply to non-heterosexual couples. For transgender people, he said you can see the gender based on self-determination. He said the whole statute was not under challenge, but only the discriminatory provisions.

Dr Singhvi then went on to attack the notice regime. He argued that the notice regime under the SMA, which requires a thirty-day public notice of intent to marriage, was unconstitutional because before a formal entry into a vital form of society, that is, marriage. The State invades privacy by asking the persons getting married to declare their intent and then invite public objections. He further argued that Section 4 said that persons cannot marry if they are underage, and people have to fulfil the conditions. He argued that so long as the conditions of marriage were met, the affidavit was tendered and the form given, and then if either spouse or the outside world has the ability to get the marriage void or voidable, that would be an invitation to violence since virtually all personal information is made public.

Singhvi finished his arguments with words by Oscar Wilde from *The Picture of Dorian Gray*.[24] He said, 'And alien tears will fill for him pity's long broken urn. For his mourners will all be outcast men, and outcasts always mourn.'

Singhvi's end with a dramatic flourish was complemented by the next counsel, Mr Raju Ramachandran. He began his arguments, attacking the idea of the 'urban elite' and why fundamental rights ought to be accorded to queer people. He quoted a judgment by one of India's finest judges, Vivian Bose, who said, 'The Constitution is not for the exclusive benefit of governments and states . . . it also exists for the common man, for the poor and the humble . . . for the butcher, the baker and the candlestick maker.'[25] He then spoke of the Randhir Singh case[26] which involved a Delhi constable who sought equal pay for equal work. Justice Chinnappa Reddy, while allowing the petition, had said:

> True, he is the merest microbe in the mighty organism of the State, a little clog in a giant wheel. But, the glory of our Constitution is that it enables him to directly approach the highest court in the land for redress. It is a matter of no little pride and satisfaction to us that he has done so. Hitherto the equality clauses of the Constitution, as other articles of the Constitution guaranteeing fundamental and other rights, were most often invoked by the privileged classes for their protection and advancement and for a 'fair and satisfactory' distribution of the buttered leaves amongst themselves. Now, thanks to the rising social and political consciousness and the expectations roused as a consequence, and the forward-looking posture of this court, the underprivileged are also clamouring for their rights and are seeking the intervention of the court with touching faith and confidence in the court.

Reading these words was a powerful way of setting the stage for his arguments. He then went on to speak about the clients that he was representing in the case. He said his client, Kajal, was a Dalit woman from Muktsar in Punjab, who lived with her partner, Bhavna, an OBC woman from Bahadurgarh, Haryana. Bhavna worked as an accountant in a company in Chandigarh and Kajal worked as an assistant in a bakery in Chandigarh. He argued that these people were not urban elites. Such a statement from the Union, he argued, was careless, unnecessary and insensitive. He said that he used the background of the petitioners only to demonstrate that the institution of marriage was not just a gateway to several rights, but one that provided societal protection from their own natal parental families. They had to move to the Delhi High Court for protection orders from their own biological families, and thus the recognition of their marriage would afford important protection to them.

Ramachandran's arguments were broadly based on the interpretation of Section 4, on fundamental rights and a challenge to the notice regime. He showed the court how Section 4 of the SMA had gender-neutral words such as: 'persons'; 'neither party'; 'the male has completed the age of twenty-one years and the female the age of eighteen years'. He argued that intending to contend that the homosexual union was contemplated or not, the language of the Act was capable of accommodating queerness without doing violence to language. He argued that the age of twenty-one could continue to operate for gay marriages, while the age of eighteen years could continue to operate for lesbian women. The issue remained for transgender persons, Justice Bhat said. Ramachandran argued that this would continue to leave out some people; he called it descriptional sacrifice. As a non-binary person who had just been sacrificed at the altar of 'legal description', I wanted to scream. But this brings me back to my point: it is virtually impossible to legally define queerness if we want to achieve liberation. Each person defines their own queerness for themselves in an ideal world and all their relationships ought to be accorded legal sanction. He spoke of how the ages of eighteen and twenty-one were rooted in a patriarchal notion—the man was the bread-earner and the female the child-bearer and they had to be those ages to be able to perform these functions.

At some point, Justice Kohli had, during the hearing, raised the issue of marriage prohibition being a restriction or a lack of recognition. Ramachandran argued that it was a lack of recognition and this lack led to the denial of equal protection of laws. He argued that the lack of protection was sufficient to create a situation of unconstitutionality which can be set aside by a queer-affirmative reading of the Act.

Right to health, and Article 21 was another argument that he used: The argument was that the right to health included the right to have appropriate medical decisions taken for an individual by the person they love. Tying it to natal family violence, he said that in the event of sickness, the individual was left without a person who could sign the hospital consent form. There was often no legal caregiver present. His second argument was that a queer person's health and happiness depended on a fulfilling union with a person of their choice. This formed an important part of mental health. He also read an argument in Article 25 and the right to conscience therein where he argued that it included a right to form one's own moral compass.

Ramachandran then spoke of the notice regime. He traced the history of the SMA. Originally, he said, there was no codified law on marriage. During British rule, there was the need felt for a marriage law for the British in India which contemplated marriage only among Christians. This need was combined with Keshav Chandra Sen and the Brahmo Samaj, and their demand for a secular law of marriage for those in the Brahmo

Samaj to marry. Since the personal law was based on religion, it required parties to renounce religions—not being a Hindu was a prerequisite. This changed in 1923 when renouncement was no longer required. He then spoke of the notice regime and its origins. It originated in the Clandestine Marriages Act of 1753 of the British Parliament which was passed to passed to prevent the celebration and solemnization of marriages outside the Church in England and Wales. It was here that the provision which originated in a preventive statute continued into the SMA, which is an enabling statute, he argued. He said that the thirty-day notice period was the longest anywhere in the world. He argued that for the exercise of a fundamental right, a person should not be required to give notice. Such a regime was not constitutional. He argued that a procedural notice was different, and at the time of registration of marriage, the marriage registrar could be present. He said that a thirty-day notice period was designed to enable parents and families to create roadblocks.

Ramachandran argued that such a postponement created a real possibility of families intervening and putting an end to the relationship and therefore it had to be struck down. The Chief Justice agreed, and said that there was a real likelihood that this would have a disproportionate effect on a spouse who belonged to a minority or a vulnerable section of society. Ramachandran brought it home, perhaps intentionally, about how this case was also about the mundanities of queer lives. He posed an interesting question. 'The notice regime requires the parties intending to marry to give a thirty-day domicile requirement before they can even give a public notice. In case of a runaway couple which has to choose a new abode before getting married, which landlord will give premises on rent for thirty to sixty days?' When Justice Kohli said that this would be true for heterosexual couples too, Ramachandran quipped that it should be struck down for all as it was a 'retrograde and obnoxious' provision. Finally, he said that there was the need for a protocol to be laid down by the court, for couples on the run from parental families need the protection of the state.

To my mind, Ramachandran had perfectly countered the criticism of the institution of marriage being taken to court, which had happened to come from those outside and inside the court. It was not about the urban elite; it was about the daily lives of 'a butcher, a baker and a candlestick maker'. It was about a couple where one partner was Dalit and the other an OBC person who had escaped family violence. It showed why marriage was a legitimate need and not a bourgeoise demand.

After Ramachandran, it was the turn of Mr K.V. Viswanathan who was representing Zainab Patel. Soon after the case, Mr Viswanathan became Hon'ble Mr Justice Viswanathan, a judge of the Supreme Court, and he is slated to become the Chief Justice of India in 2030, if all goes according to plan. Like Ramachandran, his opening was powerful. He thundered, 'If we can be daughters, brothers, sisters, brothers- and sisters-in-laws, uncles, aunts and friends after the judgment, what is it that holds us back from acquiring [the] status of married spouse. Marriage as an institution does not comply with your practices and requirements, hence we won't accommodate you in the institution of marriage. Does that have constitutional sanction?'

He then moved to the crux of his argument: The act of procreation was but one aspect of marriage. The lack of procreative abilities biologically could not prohibit parties from entering into a marriage. He then took an interesting turn: Marriage statutes, he said, do not prescribe a maximum age but only a minimum one. People beyond the age of reproduction are allowed to marry, as also are people who have decided to or cannot have children. Based on the decision in Loving v. Virginia,[27] which allowed interracial marriage in the United States, he said that marriage could not be comprehended through only a traditional lens, and that it must evolve. He said that the argument of the Union was that queer people were almost equal but separate. He argued that there were greater things in marriage: The coming together of souls and love. He then spoke of the right of transgender persons to get married. He noted how the judgment in *NALSA* guaranteed the right to marry. He then went on to speak about how the courts could mould relief.

He then attacked the view of the Union that same-sex persons should not be allowed to adopt children. If this is the view of the Union, he said, it helps the case of the petitioners for marriage so that adopted children would have a proper environment. He finally relied on a string of cases to argue that in cases of custody and adoption, it was the welfare of the child that was paramount. Homosexuals are as well suited as heterosexuals to bring up children.

With this, the third day ended. There were problematic usages such as transgender people 'leaning towards the other gender'. To which the Chief Justice reiterated that the concepts of biological man and woman were not absolute. He exclaimed that he said that at the risk of being trolled. I think this joke from the Chief Justice tells us that our judges are under extreme pressure. They ought not to be trolled to achieve an outcome, one way or the other. But vehement and strong criticism ought to be welcomed, provided that said criticism is made in good faith.

* * *

25 April: Day Four

Unlike the previous days, when there were one or two counsels addressing the court, the next two days had multiple counsels doing so, albeit briefly since most ground was covered by the previous counsels who had opened the case.

The day started with Ms Geeta Luthra opening the case. Unlike other cases which were under the SMA, the petitioners in this case were seeking recognition of their marriage under the Foreign Marriage Act, 1969, which provides for a registration of marriage between parties, one of whom has to be a citizen of India. Like the SMA, this is a secular Act. Ms Luthra referred to the 23rd Law Commission Report, which was a precursor to the FMA: She argued that marriage between an Indian citizen living abroad and a foreign citizen calls into play the concept of comity of nations which is brought in through Section 17(3) of the FMA. Simply put, comity of nations is the mutual recognition of laws and customs. Section 17(3) provides for refusal to register a marriage by the marriage officer on the ground that the marriage is inconsistent with international law or the comity of nations.

She grounded her arguments in her case's petitioners no. 1 and 2 who in her petition were legally married in Texas, United States, under valid civil law, and they had a four-month-old daughter. She spoke of their relationship, which began in 2012, and their marriage in 2017. They were equals in the US and other countries but not in the country of their origin, she said. In fact, petitioner no. 2 could not come to India during the pandemic when visas were granted to spouses of Indian citizens.

I think this was another instance of why I got involved with this litigation. I have vivid memories of the pandemic, and the queer couples who had spoken openly about not being able to visit the families of their partners. Beyond the catchy memes and pastel-shade Instagram reels, this litigation was about equality and the mundanities of love. Love is thrilling, but it is also mundane. It is sitting together on roller-coaster rides but also doing dishes together. For me, it was about the fact that cisgender heterosexual people were allowed to be a certain way, while someone like me was not.

Like other counsel before her, she too spoke of how discrimination on the grounds of sex, sexual orientation and gender of a partner was violative of Article 15 of the Constitution. She then quoted John Stuart Mill's *On Liberty*:[28]

> If all mankind minus one were of one opinion, mankind would be no more justified in silencing that one person than he, if he had the power, would be justified in silencing mankind. If all mankind had an opinion or an action, and another individual had a different opinion, mankind would not be justified in silencing that one individual just like that one individual, if given the power to do so, would not be justified in silencing all of mankind. The tendency of society is normally to impose through other means than civil penalty, its own ideas, practices and rule of conduct on those who defer from them.

This argument on liberty was a slight deviation from previous arguments which grounded it in rights. While rights required an explicit allowance and recognition of the State, the argument here seemed to be that unless there was an explicit prohibition, there should be the freedom to marry a person.

Ms Luthra argued that the heavy weight of international law principles was behind the petitioners, and that the court ought to rule in their favour. She then spoke of the notion of constitutional comity. She said fundamental rights required not just comity of nations, but constitutional comity. She backed this up with data: Twelve out of twelve of the G20 countries including the European Union have permitted same-sex marriages; thirty-four countries across the world recognize queer marriages.

Justice Bhat then wondered if civil unions were the right way to go about this, and whether jumping straight to marriages was jumping the gun. Note here that all petitions had asked for marriages, and not one had civil union as a prayer. To which Ms Luthra replied that it was late, and now the time for civil union was long past. She said that Indian jurisprudence was now cited all over the world. She said that the petitioners were only asking for one institution, marriage, and it was their fundamental right. Note this—all throughout the arguments, in their petitions, and in written submission, the demand was for marriage and marriage alone. Yet, the majority opinion convolutes this and creates a blatantly false image of what we were seeking. I have no doubts in my mind, and at the risk of inviting contempt, I say that the judgment is intellectually dishonest, logically and legally flawed.

By the time Ms Luthra finished, I was quivering and shaking: We were supposed to go next. It was the moment I had been awaiting for months now. Adrenaline coursed through my body as Mr Anand Grover got up and began his arguments. His arguments were borrowed from US jurisprudence and the doctrine of intimate association. He argued that there were two kinds of associations which can be formed under Article 19(1)(c) of the Constitution which allows citizens to form associations or unions. The first kind was known to Indian jurisprudence, namely the formation of expressive unions like cooperative societies and trade unions; the second kind was intimate associations like marriage and families bound together by love. In the US, these associations were protected by the First Amendment which protected free speech, and the Fourteenth and Nineteenth Amendments which ensured substantive due process. We relied on two judgments: First, Griswold v. Connecticut (1965) to argue that marriage is an intimate association, and second, we used other decisions like Roberts v. United States Jaycees (1984) and Obergefell v. Hodges (2015) to argue that the right to marry was a fundamental right which ought to be recognized. Justice Bhat argued that such a right could only be used as a declaration without remedy. He said that there were two parts to *Obergefell*: One was a declaration and the other was striking down the law. In order to recognize that a statute ought to be struck down or read into, there was a need to say that there existed a right of marriage.

Knowing that there was a lot of confusion around gender, sex, etc., we showed the bench the gender unicorn graphic which was created by the Trans Student Resources Centre in the United States. A reputed senior counsel who was on the other side, when passed a copy, flung it down and smirked condescendingly. Perhaps illustrations were not befitting the constitutional court. Well, we were here to queer the courts and highlight the work of incredible organizations. The second queer organization we highlighted was Pink List India, which maintains a repository of and tracks the utterances of members of Parliament on queer rights. On the eve of the hearings, it had put out a statement which said that issues of marriage equality had come up in Parliament multiple times over the past few years, and the legislature had chosen to not act on it. Thus, we argued that it was apposite for the courts to act on it.

Finally, Mr Grover argued on the issue of marriage for transgender people. Pointing out the work of exceptional scholars like Ruth Vanita and Saleem Kidwai, and the judgment in *NALSA*, he argued that queerness is a part of our tradition and was recognized in ancient India. Finally, I pulled

out a poem for him to read, one that my mother read to me
when I was a kid. It is called 'On Marriage', from *The Prophet*
by Khalil Gibran. This was a quintessential bedtime book that
my mother read to me every week. The poem goes like this:

Then Almitra spoke again and said, And
what of Marriage, master?
And he answered saying:
You were born together, and together you
shall be forevermore.
You shall be together when the white
wings of death scatter your days.
Ay, you shall be together even in the
silent memory of God.
But let there be spaces in your togetherness,
And let the winds of the heavens dance
between you.
Love one another, but make not a bond
of love:
Let it rather be a moving sea between
the shores of your souls.
Fill each other's cup but drink not from
one cup.
Give one another of your bread but eat
not from the same loaf.
Sing and dance together and be joyous,
but let each one of you be alone,
Even as the strings of a lute are alone
though they quiver with the same music.
Give your hearts, but not into each
other's keeping.
For only the hand of Life can contain
your hearts.

And stand together yet not too near
together:
For the pillars of the temple stand apart,
And the oak tree and the cypress grow
not in each other's shadow.'

As Mr Grover finished, I heaved a sigh of relief. Well begun was half done. We now had to figure out what we were arguing in rejoinder. But one thing was clear—when Mr Grover spoke, his decades' worth of work with the community was evident. The judges knew it and gave him an audience that he deserved.

Mr Grover was followed by Jayna Kothari, another senior advocate who has been a strong ally for the community both inside and outside the court. She represented transgender activist Dr Akkai Padmashali. She argued that this ought to be referred to not as the same-sex marriage case, but the marriage equality case. It was not about same-sex marriages, but about the equality of the right to marry irrespective of gender and sexual orientation.

She argued that despite the recognition of the difference between sex assigned at birth and gender in *NALSA*, transgender people were unable to exercise their legal rights. She told the court about the difficulties faced by transgender persons in changing gender identity and the perils for people who identify as neither of the binary and intersex persons.

Her next argument was based on the right to found a family under Article 21 of the Constitution of India. She then told the court the inspiring story of Akkai Padmashali, the petitioner who was assigned male at birth, faced violence at the parental home and was forced to leave the birth family when she was fourteen or fifteen years old. She spent years on the streets begging and now had a PhD.

Kothari argued that the right to marry had been recognized by the Supreme Court, but the right to marry gives rise to a family, which was also a right that needed to be protected under Article 21. She then spoke of marriages and families, which may be with or without children, and the concept of families which goes to the core of our being. These are required for love and care and psychological and economic support and is a basic unit of society we turn back to in troubling times. She pointed out that transgender persons were marrying and having children, but they were not enjoying this right—marriage is not a heterosexual institution. She spoke of the atypical manifestations of the family, which the Supreme Court had held deserved the protection of the law. She grounded her arguments in the Universal Declaration of Human Rights, *Yogyakarta Principles* and various cases from around the world.

Her argument was that the SMA denied transgender persons the right to marry and have a family and was unconstitutional. She spoke of Article 15(1) of the Constitution which prohibited discrimination on the basis of sex, which has now been expanded to gender.

Based on this argument, she argued that that the sections of the SMA which read 'man' and 'woman' be replaced with the word 'persons', and the words 'husband' and 'wife' be replaced with the word 'spouses.'

Next in line was Menaka Guruswamy, who had spearheaded this litigation in the Delhi High Court, along with Saurabh Kirpal and Arundhati Katju. Guruswamy was appearing in two cases: The first was Aditi Anand v. Union of India, which involved a challenge to the SMA, and secondly, an intervention by the Delhi Commission for Protection of Child Rights (DCPCR) which supported the issue of adoption by queer couples.

First, she argued that the Indian Constitution had a form of constrained parliamentary supremacy. She argued that

Parliament was not supreme, like in England, as the Union made it out to be, but it was a creature of the Constitution, and thus bound by it. The Chief Justice disagreed—the canvas covered by these petitions, he argued, fell within the domain of Parliament and that was undisputed. Drawing attention to Entry 5 of List 3 of Schedule VII, he said that Parliament had jurisdiction on the issue. So he posed a question before Guruswamy: If this was a power conferred especially on Parliament, which are those openings which the court can explore? He was pointing to the separation of powers between the two branches of the government.

Justice Bhat added it and said that there was an obligation on lawmakers, such as under Article 17 which prohibits untouchability and makes it an offence but was inadequate, the Court did not step in by enacting a law that criminalized it. He said there has to be a right included in the law for there to be a remedy. To which Guruswamy showed how the phraseology of Article 17 made it incumbent upon the legislature to bring in an Act. Justice Bhat then said that if there was no obligation, how could a court weave out an obligation or a mandate?

Dr Guruswamy said that Article 17 mandated the enactment of a law and hence the words used were 'punishable in accordance with law'. Similarly, in Article 21A of the Constitution (the Right to Education Act), Chief Justice Kapadia made a point that even pre-21A, the courts had been actively involved in implementing and advancing the right to education. She alluded to the Supreme Court being the north star for LGBTQ rights and many other facets of fundamental rights, and this was done even without the legislature walking the talk. She said that what the petitioners were asking for was not anything new, but a workable interpretation of the SMA. She argued that if it were a question of reading 'spouse' instead of 'husband' and 'wife', and if it was the question of rereading the Act, there were options available. The petitioners, she said, were only asking for a constitutionally tenable interpretation. The Union said it had a legitimate state interest (LSI) in restricting these marriages. Nine judges in *Puttuswamy* had interpreted legitimate state interests as national security, crime, innovation and dissipation of social welfare benefits. This showed when the State could claim a legitimate interest. Nowhere did the State meet this requirement. She finally ended this leg of her argument by saying that marriage included a bouquet of rights, including rights such as pension, gratuity and provident fund, and pointed out how even the pension of Supreme Court judges was premised on a spousal relationship created by marriage.

In her final leg of arguments, where she held the brief for the DCPCR, she showed various studies on how the lack of marriage affected queer kids. Her arguments were met with extreme resistance from the bench, mostly Justices Chandrachud and Bhat. But Dr Guruswamy stood firm in the face of this opposition and said again that once there was a declaration in favour of the SMA, other rights would follow.

She was followed by Senior Advocate Saurabh Kirpal, who has not been made a judge of the Delhi High Court despite a recommendation and a reiteration from the collegium for the sole reason that he is gay. Unlike the other counsels, who had impressed the implications of this case on the judges, Kirpal chose to bring it back. He said it might mean a lot for the lawyers, it might mean a lot to the people in the community, but at the end of the day, it was a dispute that the court would have to decide.

At the outset, he differentiated between parliamentary functioning and judicial review. He conceded that it was for Parliament to legislate, but this case was about marriage equality, which subsumed within it an important facet of the right to equality, namely that homosexuals and heterosexuals were equal. He said that if the court found a violation of Article 14, it would have to strike down the SMA.

He argued that under-inclusion was permitted in some cases by the legislature, but it could not ever be done on the ground of sexual orientation. Under-inclusion refers to omitting a group from the purview of a legislation by virtue of the fact that it is not equal to the people covered by the Act. Kirpal argued that any Act which excluded people solely on the ground of sexual orientation would have to be struck down as being unconstitutional, and that would be like throwing the baby out with the bathwater.

At this point, Justice Bhat asked him if his argument was an extension of that of Rohatgi's: Namely that the court must first acknowledge and attribute the exclusion of homosexual or queer couples within the SMA, then the next step would be to argue that such exclusion leads to the law being invalid constitutionally to the extent of under-inclusion. To save it, Bhat asked, wasn't the court being told to take too many legislative steps? He then told Kirpal that the petitioners had sought to bring in contemporary intention, but the intention was something else when it was enacted. While this was a broad statement, he was alluding to the fact that the court could have allowed such evolution of intention and read it into the Act. Finally, he asked Kirpal to show him an analogous instance where under-classification had been invalidated.

Kirpal replied that the argument was a classical four-step process of interpretation or striking down statutes. Every time the court reads down a statute for being under-inclusive, there had to be a finding of invalidity. He argued that to that extent the Act is void, and you have to save it from invalidity. The petitioners were attributing an inconsistency to the statute because it required an examination of the effects doctrine. He argued that any provision's effect on the lives of the people must be seen when adjudicating on its validity, which is a settled principle of law. He argued that by refusing to recognize queer marriages, and the failure of recognition of queer relationships by giving it the sanctity of law, there was a direct effect on the dignity of all queer individuals. This was directly hit by Article 14.

He added that the law said that only two heterosexual people could marry, and the direct consequence was that homosexuals could not marry. He said that the judicial process could not work in a way that the consequences of a decision precluded the bench from making one.

The Chief Justice asked again if the intention of the lawmakers while enacting the SMA was to exclude same-sex couples. Kripal replied in the negative. The Chief Justice then again posed a counterquestion: In the Hindu Code Bill, could someone who did not belong to the Hindu community say that because equality is recognized only in the bill, this violates Article 14? Kirpal again replied in the negative. He argued that there must be an underlying basis for the right to claim equality. He said that the court must first find a fundamental right to marry. If they did so, then there must be a simultaneous proportionality which must be tested in terms of balancing the statute with Articles 14, 19 and 21. Any person could not knock on the doors of the court and claim the right to equality unless prior decisions had found such a right. He said that if someone was given a right and others were denied the right, only then could there be unconstitutionality. Or, in other words, the right must have been found prior to the claim to equality.

Kirpal then argued that there was a constitutional obligation on the court. If they had found a right, that is, the fundamental right to marry, then the right could not be defeated merely because of the fact that the consequence would involve a legislative exercise. This was a dangerous precedent where rights could be trumped and defaced by complicated statutes. Lambasting the other side's argument, he said that it merely amounted to the fact that because the finding of such a right would make the job of the legislature difficult, the court must not grant such a right. He said that there was no greater anathema to the Constitution than this. In the last segment of his arguments, he pointed out that in the past seventy-five years, Parliament had not acted, and thus the argument could not be allowed or countenanced. If this was difficult, or if the court found that there was a right, it must adopt a workability model to ensure that the rights were protected.

Finally, Kirpal spoke of lavender marriages, where a gay man or a lesbian woman was forced into a heterosexual marriage and ended up ruining two lives. As someone who knows multiple people who are in such marriages as well as having dealt with cases where one party has been queer and in a lavender marriage, I could not agree more.

The final argument for the day was by Vrinda Grover who was representing various lesbian, bisexual and transgender activists, some of whom had to be anonymized due to the threat to their lives. Like other petitions, this petition also challenged the notice regime under the SMA on the patterns of marginalization and discrimination. However, what separated it from the rest was that it was based on the anti-caste and feminist critique of the institution of marriages, namely the perpetuation of caste endogamy and the control exercised over the bodies and lives of women through patriarchy. Pointing to the provisions of the Transgender Persons (Protection of Rights) Act, 2019, necessitates that the SMA provides recognition to trans persons and the other partner on the fact that it unequivocally prevented any form of discrimination under Section 3.

What separated this petition from the rest was the data and testimony of more than thirty people who had testified on the nature of violence from their birth and natal families. To that end, the petitioners here wanted a recognition of the families that they considered to be their own. She said that there was a need for such recognition for multiple reasons. She said that they wanted to put their chosen families on advance directives, or in simple terms, to specify by name individuals who were nominees not just in the estate but also to make end-of-life decisions. She argued that there must be a protocol which was adopted in the previous judgment of the Supreme Court in *Shakti Vahini*[29] to protect couples from violence from *khap* panchayats. Since I have alluded to the protocol earlier too, I think it is time to reproduce it here for the sake of the reader:

I. Preventive Steps:-

a. The state governments should forthwith identify districts, sub-divisions and/or villages where instances of honour killing or assembly of khap panchayats have been reported in the recent past, e.g., in the last five years.

b. The secretary, home department of the concerned states shall issue directives/advisories to the superintendent of police of the concerned districts for ensuring that the officer in charge of the police stations of the identified areas is extra-cautious if any instance of inter-caste or interreligious marriage within their jurisdiction comes to their notice.

c. If information about any proposed gathering of a khap panchayat comes to the knowledge of any police officer or any officer of the district administration, he shall forthwith inform his immediate superior officer and also simultaneously intimate the jurisdictional deputy superintendent of police and superintendent of police.

d. On receiving such information, the deputy superintendent of police (or such senior police officer as identified by the state governments with respect to the area/district) shall immediately interact with the members of the khap panchayat and impress upon them that convening of such [a] meeting/gathering is not permissible in law and to eschew from going ahead with such a meeting. Additionally, he should issue appropriate directions to the officer in charge of the jurisdictional police station to be vigilant and, if necessary, to deploy adequate police force for prevention of assembly of the proposed gathering.

e. Despite taking such measures, if the meeting is conducted, the deputy superintendent of police shall personally remain present during the meeting and impress upon the assembly that no decision can be taken to cause any harm to the couple or the family members of the couple, failing which each one participating in the meeting besides the organizers would be personally liable for criminal prosecution. He shall also ensure that video recording of the discussion and participation of the members of the assembly is done on the basis of which the law-enforcing machinery can resort to suitable action.

f. If the deputy superintendent of police, after interaction with the members of the khap panchayat, has reason to believe that the gathering cannot be prevented and/or is likely to cause harm to the couple or members of their family, he shall forthwith submit a proposal to the district magistrate/sub-divisional magistrate of the district/competent authority of the concerned area for issuing orders to take preventive steps under the CrPC [Criminal Procedure Code], including by invoking prohibitory orders under Section 144 CrPC and also by causing arrest of the participants in the assembly under Section 151 CrPC.

g. The home department of the Government of India must take initiative and work in coordination with the state governments to sensitize the law enforcement agencies by involving all the stake holders to identify the measures for the prevention of such violence and to implement the constitutional goal of social justice and the rule of law.

h. There should be an institutional machinery with the necessary coordination of all the stakeholders. The different state governments and the Centre ought to work on sensitization of law enforcement agencies to mandate social initiatives and awareness to curb such violence.

II. Remedial Measures:

a. Despite the preventive measures taken by the state police, if it comes to the notice of the local police that the khap panchayat has taken place and it has passed any diktat to take action against a couple/family of an inter-caste or inter-religious marriage (or any other marriage which does not meet their acceptance), the jurisdictional police official shall cause to immediately lodge an FIR under the appropriate provisions of the Indian Penal Code including Sections 141, 143, 503 read with 506 of IPC.

b. Upon registration of FIR, intimation shall be simultaneously given to the superintendent of police/deputy superintendent of police who, in turn, shall ensure that effective investigation of the crime is done and taken to its logical end with promptitude.

c. Additionally, immediate steps should be taken to provide security to the couple/family and, if necessary, to remove them to a safe house within the same district or elsewhere keeping in mind their safety and threat perception. The state government may consider of establishing a safe house at each district headquarter for that purpose. Such safe houses can cater to accommodate:

   i. Young bachelor–bachelorette couples whose relationship is being opposed by their families/local community/khaps and (ii) Young married couples (of an inter-caste or inter-religious or any other marriage being opposed by their families/local community/khaps). Such safe houses may be placed under the supervision of the jurisdictional district magistrate and superintendent of police.

d. The district magistrate/superintendent of police must deal with the complaint regarding threat administered to such couple/family with utmost sensitivity. It should be first ascertained whether the bachelor–bachelorette are capable adults. Thereafter, if necessary, they may be provided logistical support for solemnizing their marriage and/or for being duly registered under police protection, if they so desire. After the marriage, if the couple so desire, they can be provided accommodation on payment of nominal charges in the safe house initially for a period of one month to be extended on a monthly basis but not exceeding one year in aggregate, depending on their threat assessment on a case-to-case basis.

e. The initial inquiry regarding the complaint received from the couple (bachelor–bachelorette or a young married couple) or upon receiving information from an independent source that the relationship/marriage of such couple is opposed by their family members/local community/khaps shall be entrusted by the district magistrate/superintendent of police to an officer of the rank of additional superintendent of police. He shall conduct a preliminary inquiry and ascertain the authenticity, nature and gravity of threat perception. On being satisfied as to the authenticity of such threats, he shall immediately submit a report to the superintendent of police in not later than one week.

f. The district superintendent of police, upon receipt of such report, shall direct the deputy superintendent of police in charge of the concerned sub-division to cause to register an FIR against the persons threatening the couple(s) and, if necessary, invoke Section 151 of CrPC. Additionally, the deputy superintendent of police shall personally supervise the progress of investigation and ensure that the same is completed and taken to its logical end with promptitude. In the course of investigation, the concerned persons shall be booked without any exception including the members who have participated in the assembly. If the involvement of the members of [the] khap panchayat comes to the fore, they shall also be charged for the offence of conspiracy or abetment, as the case may be.

III. Punitive Measures:

a. Any failure by either the police or district officer/officials to comply with the aforesaid directions shall be considered as an act of deliberate negligence and/or misconduct for which departmental action must be taken under the service rules. The departmental action shall be initiated and taken to its logical end, preferably not exceeding six months, by the authority of the first instance.

b. In terms of the ruling of this court in Arumugam Servai (supra), the states are directed to take disciplinary action against the concerned officials if it is found that (i) such official(s) did not prevent the incident, despite having prior knowledge of it, or (ii) where the incident had already occurred, such official(s) did not promptly apprehend and institute criminal proceedings against the culprits.

c. The state governments shall create special cells in every district comprising of the superintendent of police, the district social welfare officer and district Adi-Dravidar welfare officer to receive petitions/complaints of harassment of and threat to couples of inter-caste marriage.

d. These special cells shall create a 24-hour helpline to receive and register such complaints and to provide necessary assistance/advice and protection to the couple.

e. The criminal cases pertaining to honour killing or violence to the couple(s) shall be tried before the designated court/fast track court earmarked for that purpose. The trial must proceed on day to day basis to be concluded preferably within six months from the date of taking cognizance of the offence. We may hasten to add that this direction shall apply even to pending cases. The concerned district judge shall assign those cases, as far as possible, to one jurisdictional court so as to ensure expeditious disposal thereof.

Grover also argued that agency of consenting adults has to be protected and for the creation of safe houses and shelter homes. Justice Bhat raised the issues of recognition of hijra gharanas, which was an important intervention. This was a brilliant argument where the law was mixed with research, anecdotes and the lived realities of queer lives. This was a shift from focusing on marginalization to focusing on ways in which queer people can recreate their joys in their own ways.

Day four ended with a cavalcade of senior counsels addressing the court, and there were still a few which were left for the fifth day.

* * *

26 April: Day Five

The final day for the arguments of the petitioners was here. So far, the hearings were broadly looking as if the judges, though cynical, were in our favour, despite the steep resistance that we were met with on how to interpret the SMA. Little did we know that in the post-lunch session, the tables would have flipped, and our case placed on shaky ground.

The fifth day began with arguments by Ms Karuna Nundy representing clients who wanted recognition of their marriage under the SMA. Her arguments sought a declaration to include the rights of queer and non-heterosexual persons under both the SMA, as also the FMA. Her argument was that the rights for transgender persons which emanated from the decision in *NALSA* recognized a wide range of marriages between persons of diverse identities, which she argued was deliberate. Her final argument was that the word in *NALSA* to describe queer persons as 'third-gender spouses' would include non-binary persons. Therefore, her argument was that the phrase 'third-gender spouse' should be read along with the words 'husband' and 'wife' in the SMA.

Nundy was followed by Arundhati Katju, who began her arguments by conceding that the issues before the court were complex and told the courts the extent to which they could interpret the statutes.

For non-lawyers who may be reading this, the interpretation of statutes is the process by which the courts, in India and around the world, interpret and apply a statutory provision to the case at hand. I have repeated and reiterated that the law abhors chaos—it is through the process of interpretation of statutes that it tries to bring order to human life. The law cannot foresee and create a rule for every situation. So the process of interpretation is often used by the court to bring a situation that the law did not foresee into the existing rules. For this, often, strange cases come before the court. For example, one of the famous cases that came up before the Authority for Advance Ruling, which decides matters of the Goods and Services Tax, was: Is 'paratha' a 'roti'?[30] This came up before the authority because paratha was taxed at 18 per cent while roti was taxed at 5 per cent. The court had to interpret what a paratha was, what a roti was, and then distinguish between them.

Katju then told the court that it had to read into the statute and expand the statute to include an excluded class, and such a reading had to be done in order to update the statute in terms of a present-day understanding of social norms and the Constitution. She showed the court the various ways in which the heterosexual community had gone through an organic process of filing claims which were adjudicated by the court, and it was this parity that queer couples were also seeking.

She argued that every question would not be decided in this case. The statutes were complex, and the courts would be approached again and again, and the interpretation of statutes would come up before the court. She posited that despite the codification of personal laws since the 1800s, heterosexual couples continue to come to the courts and seek interpretation and protection from unconstitutional provisions, and this itself made a strong case for why the SMA should apply to queer couples, as it did to other couples.

A mere declaration, whether negative or positive, or a mandamus prohibition of discrimination, would go a long way in nudging the government to commence the work.

The next question that Katju pontificated over was the intersection of the secular law of the SMA with the personal law of the HMA. A prima facie reading of the SMA would make it seem like it is a secular law. But it is not. Vide an amendment in 1976, Section 21A was inserted in the SMA, whereby when a person professing the Hindu, Buddhist, Sikh or Jain religion married a person who professes the Hindu, Buddhist, Sikh or Jain religion, then Sections 19, 20 (insofar as it creates a disability) and 21 did not apply.

Section 19 creates a severance from the Hindu Undivided Family for a person who professes the Hindu, Buddhist, Sikh or Jain religion if they married another person under the SMA. Section 21A creates an exception provided that the other party also professes the Hindu, Buddhist, Sikh or Jain religion, and allows them to inherit ancestral family property. Section 20 allows, subject to the provisions of Section 19, any person who marries under the SMA to have the same rights and be subject to the same disabilities in regard to the right of succession to any property as a person to whom the Caste Disabilities Removal Act, 1850 (21 of 1850), applies. Section 21 says that persons who are married under the SMA shall be covered by the Indian Succession Act which is a secular law for succession.

This is a fairly complex bit of legalese, and the best way to untangle legal knots is through illustrations. The best illustration is provided by Saptarshi Mandal in a piece titled 'Can Judges Deliver Marriage Equality?' He writes:

Suppose the SMA is interpreted to recognize same-sex marriage, as the petitioners have asked, allowing two Hindu men, Prince and Lucky, to have a valid civil marriage. But by virtue of Section 21A, both of them will continue to be governed by the Hindu Succession Act (HSA). Let us say, Lucky dies, without making a will. As per the HSA, his self-acquired property as well as his interest in a coparcenary will now devolve upon his heirs [Sections 6(3) and 8 read with the Schedule]. But for a Hindu male, the HSA recognizes only his 'widow' i.e., his female spouse, to be an heir, consistent with the definition of a valid marriage under the HMA, which means that despite being married to Lucky, Prince will not be treated as a spouse for the purpose of succession. Thus, the difficulty with recognizing same-sex marriage under the SMA is that it will make Section 21A of the Act inoperative—something which even the most liberal theories of statutory interpretation do not allow. The only way out of this problem is if same-sex marriage

is also recognized under the HMA, which is the subject
matter of another set of petitions.[31]

Note here that some of us had foreseen this problem and
had thus filed petitions under both the HMA and the SMA.
However, we were limited by the court, which perhaps did
not want to open a can of worms of religious opposition to
recognition of queer marriages under religious personal laws.
Day after day, the Supreme Court is becoming increasingly
aware of its limited political capital and trying to do things
only incrementally. This has not boded well for our democracy
and the Supreme Court has come under severe criticism
from right-thinking citizens and public intellectuals.

Justice Bhat then asked Katju if she was presupposing
that there would be same-sex couples in the same religion and
whether 21A would apply to interfaith couples also. Katju
replied that she was aware that there were interfaith couples,
so 21A would not apply.

Katju then went on to trace the legislative history of the
SMA, pointing out that when it comes to the application
of laws, they must be uniform for all couples. She reiterated
that there was no need to interpret it in a gender-neutral
couple. She said marriage was, amongst other things, also a
gateway for couples to adopt kids. Pointing out that not all
couples procreate, nor does the law mandate bearing children
naturally, she pointed out how a child born through adoption
or surrogacy had the same rights.

She finally ended with a prayer that there should be a
twofold declaration: A positive one which recognizes queer
marriage, and a negative one which prohibits discrimination.

Katju was followed by Amritananda Chakraborty, whose
clients were challenging the provisions of the SMA, and were
the only persons to have challenged adoption regulations.

Chakraborty pointed out how the petitioners were married for fifteen years and also married under the law of Denmark in August 2022. They wished to settle in India and wanted a recognition of their marriage.

She argued that had it not been for their sexual orientation, the petitioners would have had their marriage recognized under the SMA. The petitioners were in Denmark on professional deputation, but they wanted to come back and live their lives in India. This non-recognition, she argued, was not under-inclusion, but discrimination, plain and simple, which could not be countenanced by the Constitution.

A major chunk of Chakraborty's eloquent arguments was focused on adoption regulations. She pointed out how the Juvenile Justice Act while speaking of prospective parents used the word 'persons' or 'person'. She showed how marital status was not a criterion for the eligibility to adopt. She pointed out how the Act used the words 'couple' or 'spouse', but since only heterosexuals were permitted to marry, it precluded homosexual couples from adopting. Marriage became a precondition to other rights, which the Supreme Court had struck down as being unconstitutional when a woman was not given an abortion because of her marital status.[32] She said that this defeated the very purpose of adoption which was to provide children with love and care. She also framed her argument in a different way from counsels who had argued hitherto: Children who were orphaned, abandoned and surrendered also had a right to family. Excluding transgender persons and persons who are queer amounted to the denial of a right to those children also.

Multiple other counsels followed Chakraborty with brief submissions, and the bench rose for lunch as the petitioners finished their arguments.

As you read this chapter and the others following this, I do want to highlight one thing. I write this after the judgment was delivered with the benefit of hindsight. Counsels who argue the case have to think on their feet and have a legal strategy ready. They lack the luxury of time which those of us who are not arguing but analysing with the benefit of hindsight and time to reflect. The arguments and the analysis of this chapter are based on revisiting the recordings, the transcripts and my own notes from the court during every day of the proceedings. There may be a harsh critique or two but that is not meant to run down either the counsel or their arguments but to appeal to a future generation who may argue cases. There are some problems which are systemic, such as some counsels being given more time than others, for which I am too junior to provide solutions.

So far, we had seen queer euphoria, queer anger, queer plight in the court, and the assertion of queer identities. From Justice Singhvi asking if there were queer people in court during the hearings in Suresh Kumar Koshal, to multiple counsels, both who argued and those that assisted in Supriyo Chakraborty, we had come a long way. Being in that court, playing a tiny role in the battery of lawyers, was still nothing short of enthralling and exhilarating. Little did we know what was coming towards us in the next few days. Our lives were going to be reduced to a circus, of amorphous identities which had to be brought into social and legal conformity.

Chapter 5

Macabre and Malice

The men believe that activity results from frustration and frustration results from never being able to get what you want. The perpetual out-of-reach. The men frantically scurry about with great schemes and much noise to try and reach the out-of-reach. Each tries to be the first or richest or strongest or most potent. Each compares himself to the others and each is always inadequate; less than first, not yet rich enough, or strong enough, or potent enough. None of this leads to happiness, but then the men do not look approvingly at happiness. None of this leads to contentment but then the men care nothing for contentment. They fill their heads with inflated notions of total control and empire and strength and sexual conquest. They fill their bodies with meat and drugs and dirty air. And they rush about in a frenzy making messes and ugliness and fear everywhere. And when they tire they sit with each other and lament and blabber how little they are appreciated and how hard they try and how nothing ever works out quite as they plan.
—Larry Mitchell, *The Faggots and Their Friends Between Revolutions*[1]

Now that the petitioners had finished, it was time to brace ourselves, for it was the respondents, who represented the Union of India, various state governments including Gujarat, Madhya Pradesh, Odisha, religious groups, and even one group that supposedly works on trafficking issues, who were to argue now. We knew sitting through this would not be easy, and that our lives would be used to flame culture wars and sound dogwhistles to the audience watching the proceedings online We had little that we could do, for both sides were to be heard. We did not have a simple case. Yet, we knew that the arguments of the respondents were going to reduce us to mere deviants and would refuse to see humanity beyond identity. And so, after lunch on the fifth day, the Solicitor General, Mr Tushar Mehta, began his arguments.

26 April: Day Five, Post-Lunch Session

Mehta started his arguments by creating alarm. He began by saying that this case would have a huge social impact, and reiterated his earlier prayer to leave the issue for Parliament to decide. He acquiesced that there was a Constitution bench decision in *Navtej* which had held that there was a fundamental right to sexual orientation, which was read into our Constitution by the court, and that was not disputed. Nor was the union disputing the right to non-discrimination or personal autonomy. He said that the prayer for marriage was the creation of a social institution, and contested the right of the court to decide what constitutes marriage and between which parties. He argued that there would be unintended consequences such as differences between civil society groups and different state legislatures. He argued that there needed to be a national debate on the laws and their implications; there were 160 provisions which would be affected by several laws, and it would be a mammoth task for the court to indulge in. He argued that there was an issue for the legislature to decide. He said marriage is always between 'a conventional man and a conventional woman', meaning thereby between a cis man and a cis woman.

He then went on to say that there was no value judgement of queer persons, and he said that Parliament had recognized all the rights laid down in terms of choice, sexual autonomy, 'sexual preference' (by which he meant orientation) and privacy. He said there was no stigma. When the Solicitor General argued that there was no stigma, my whole life flashed before me. All the bullying, all the jeering, all the judgmental looks. Arvey Malhotra. Avinshu Patel. Anjana Harish. If there was no stigma, what led to these deaths? What led to me being bullied? What led to the Solicitor General saying 'man means man' to the Chief Justice on an earlier date? These are questions perhaps that no one except the Solicitor General himself could answer.

He then argued that the right to marry does not compel the State to create a new definition of marriage. He said that such a right was for Parliament to decide, but it was not an absolute right. He argued that some parts could only be taken care of by Parliament. Note here that under no statute is marriage defined. The law only tells us who can enter a marriage, the process of marrying and the process of exiting a marriage through divorce. So where does the definition of marriage come from? I firmly believe that is up to the parties to a marriage to decide and define their marriage. The Solicitor General then said that societal acceptance was the only recognition post the 1956 HMA. He argued that with legislative approval, there was to be a regulatory provision. He said it was only Parliament that could conceive of the situations of potential problems.

He then took the court to the SMA, and showed how the recognition was seemingly between conventional man and conventional woman. Note here that there is no place where the word 'conventional' is used in the SMA. He argued that the request of the petitioners was to rewrite the SMA to suit their situation, to which he was not opposed, but it was for Parliament to decide. The issue of queer marriages was consciously omitted under the SMA.

The Solicitor General proposed that there were some constraints on the courts, namely that it cannot change the character of the law, it cannot substitute the manifest legislative intent, it cannot read words of a larger amplitude into words of a smaller amplitude. He said this would have unintended consequences on heterosexual couples. At this point, Justice Bhat interjected and asked if there could be different lenses of interpretation which could be used for heterosexual and non-heterosexual couples. To this, the Solicitor General replied that it would be impossible to reconcile the differences and the impact of such an interpretation.

Then—and I do not make this up—he took the court through what LGBTQIA+ stood for. He then said that '+' was going to be the source of the problem. He said there were seventy-two different shades and spectrums which would arise, and that the court could not go into all of them. He said this was an 'unidentified group' of persons. How could the court reconcile it? Then he presented the court with a table which had various definitions of genders, few of which I or anyone I knew had not heard of, including one that said 'gender changes according to mood swings'. This was done to reduce our lives and lived experiences to a joke, to turn us into unregulated subjects of the law who must be brought into conformity through a legislative diktat. He then posed a question: If two parties got married, what would be the source of 'testing their gender' at the time of divorce? Since the SMA provided for different grounds of divorce for a husband and for his wife. He said that there was not a prohibition of marriage; people were free to marry. What was prohibited was the conferment of a legal status. He said these were social institutes which predated statutes, and thus societal recognition must necessarily flow for legal recognition.

He then said that a husband and wife complete each other and after marriage they are transformed into a new entity, and this was not an archaic concept. He argued that marriage, as it was recognized, either as a sacrament or a contract, was only between heterosexuals. It was based on mutual consent between a man and a woman which was common to each religious tradition even if they were represented by parents or guardians. Heterosexual marriages, the Solicitor General argued, were ordained by religious practices for the furtherance of society and orderly influence of persons in society.

The Solicitor General then argued that the prayers were vague, and the recognition of marriage as a social institution was a job for the legislature. He said when the petitioners wanted a confirmation of their supposed pre-existing rights, it was for the judges who were free to decide as they saw fit, but still bound by the shackles of judicial discipline of separation of powers, and this was the nature of the judicial process. He said the judges were not supposed to yield to 'spasmodic sentiment to vague and unregulated benevolence'. It would be a completely vague declaration even if such a declaration was granted by the court because of the problems that would occur. He then went on to the dissent in *Obergefell* where the court was criticized for acting as super legislature, and argued that apart from the text of the statute, nothing more could be read into it. He said that judges had to decide cases as they come, without taking into consideration their own prejudices and biases, and there could not be a blind adherence to such a verdict which could be compelled.

He then argued that a legislation did not become unlawful because it had any other alternative, mostly in social and economic laws. It was the legislative policy that the marriage was between heterosexual couples. It could only be reconsidered by Parliament.

The Solicitor General then went on to cite the United States decision in *Dobbs*, which essentially held that there was no right to abortion in the US. He read out passages from *Dobbs* where the court had held that this was an issue which ought to be returned to elected representatives. He was stopped short by the Chief Justice. Arguing that the limits of judicial power were well settled, the Chief Justice countered it by saying that there was no effective reliance that could be placed as we were ahead in time and the decision held that women had no bodily autonomy in the US. Mehta replied that he was not a fan of citing *Dobbs*. To which the Chief Justice argued that *Dobbs* could certainly not be cited. Mehta shot back that he was not relying on *Dobbs* for what it said with respect to autonomy but on the limited issue of limitations on judicial power.

He argued then that the court was not confronted with a law that prohibited same-sex relationships, and said that *Ghaidan* was cited out of context. He said the foundational distinction was that it was given in the context of tenancy, and thus could not be relied upon. He argued that it would not apply to the Indian context. He then took the court through various countries and how they recognized marriages through legislation, and argued that South Africa was the only country where marriage equality was initiated by the judiciary. This was an incorrect statement. This was also done in Taiwan, is being done in Japan as we speak, and even the American Court of Human Rights in South America.

He then went on to counter Rohatgi's submission that the statute did not recognize non-heterosexual relationships. Mehta argued that this was not a mistake, but a conscious omission. He took the court through various documents and debates by the Minister and members of Parliament to argue that queer marriages were left out consciously.

With this, the clock struck four, and the judges rose. We were halfway through this fight, and still had five days to go.

* * *

27 April: Day Six

Like the previous day, the Solicitor General began the next morning. He is often mistaken by a lot of people to be a bad lawyer. They misjudge him. Despite my vehement disagreements with him, there is no denying that he has been effective advocate for the government in court, which by most accounts, has been the most sway that any law officer has had in the institutional memory of the Supreme Court. He's a master of his craft; like an expert actor, he designs each role in each case in a way that will suit the stand that the government takes. The act in this case was tailored not for the consumption of judges, but for the public at large since the court proceedings were being live-streamed. Here, he did that by employing harmful language and distasteful and inaccurate comparisons.

He began his arguments again by talking about restrictions on the right to marry for incestuous relationships—reductio ad absurdum, or stretching an argument to its most absurd stage. Or, as logicians call them, apagogical arguments. If I were attracted to my sister, and we were both consenting adults who claimed the right of autonomy and choice, could we marry each other? He asked the bench this. Bhat took the bait and said that there was nothing which was absolutely private even within marriage. The Solicitor General said that this was what the petitioners were arguing. But it was a straw-man argument. We were in court exactly to get the State to regulate our marriages. The Chief Justice cut this short by interjecting that this was an extreme statement. Mehta then read out definitions of relatives by full blood and half blood.

Showing a list of various provisions, which amounted to around 160 in number, he asked the bench a rhetorical question. Who would be the wife in a marriage between two men and two women? Now a perfect interpretation was possible for the limited purposes of this question. In a gay marriage, only grounds that are available to the husbands would be used, while in a lesbian marriage, the grounds of divorce which are available to the wife should be used. He then took the court to Section 31 of the SMA which provides for a place where the courts may be approached for the purposes of a divorce petition. He argued that it was usually where the wife resided. He said that the court would be faced with several such questions. Who would claim maintenance since it was only the wife who could claim it?

The answer to this in my opinion is also simple. The wife is a vulnerable party in a marriage and can thus claim maintenance. When a petition for maintenance is filed, the court should analyse if the party claiming maintenance is less vulnerable between the two, and then decide whether to pay maintenance or not. He argued that under Section 39A of the SMA which provided for enforcing order and decree, there were different provisions for male and female.

At this juncture, the Chief Justice said that the court was faced with three issues: It was being asked to rewrite some provisions, ignore some provisions which were introduced as a matter of public policy, and finally, reinterpret personal laws since there are segments under the SMA which contain references to personal law. The Solicitor General replied that there was a fourth issue also: Whether a court could read a statute to make it applicable for different classes of society, which would make room for several complications which the court could not ignore. He demonstrated how under the Indian Succession Act, a wife's domicile during the marriage follows the domicile of the husband.

Even though personal laws were not under challenge, and the bench had said that it would not deal with issues under the personal laws, Mehta took up Sections 12 and 13 of the Hindu Adoption Act which had different eligibility criteria for adoption for males and females. He argued that such provisions could not be read in a gender-neutral fashion. He took the bench then to the laws of inheritance and how the Hindu law treats men and women differently on marriage. Could the bench read it in a gender-neutral fashion, he asked.

Justice Kaul, who had so far been relatively quiet on the bench, asked if sex was taken into consideration instead of gender, could gay marriage be facilitated? Mehta replied again that the legislature only legislated for a conventional man and woman. He added that it could not be ignored and that all same-sex couples were not before the court as petitioners. This was a specious argument. In cases of fundamental rights, even the violation of the rights of one person is enough for the court to step in. Minuscule minority jurisprudence had long been abandoned.

His next leg of argument was based on the Domestic Violence Act where the aggrieved person was a woman and the respondent any adult male who had been in a domestic relationship with the aggrieved person. He showed the court the Dowry Prohibition Act where the terms used were 'bride' and 'bridegroom'. The Solicitor General then showed the gendered provisions for a decree of judicial separation and where such a decree has to be executed.

The sum and thrust of this argument were that different classes of people can be treated differently under the same act, and that the provisions were so gendered that it would be unworkable no matter how fine the judicial craftsmanship.

He then went on to attack submissions on the House of Lords' decision in Ghaidan v. Godin-Mendoza (2004). Some petitioners had relied on the decision in *Ghaidan* to argue that 'when there is a particular paradigm that applies to the heterosexual group, it is discriminatory to not apply the same to homosexual groups'. The Solicitor General argued that this was a tenancy dispute concerning a rental enactment and did not involve the creation of a new social institution. He argued that the court could not read outside the intent of the makers of the law or the 'grain of the law', and that the process of interpretation ended where the legislation ended. He added that in Britain, Parliament was supreme and there used to be no judicial examination; the provision would only be incompatible. He argued that in India, the courts can declare a legislation illegal. If the UK courts decided that the statute was declared to be incompatible, it continued to be in force and a declaration of incompatibility did not affect the validity of the statute, and its continued operation or legality of the statute. He argued that the powers there were advisory, and the courts nudged the legislature.

The bench rose for lunch. During the lunch break, someone had told us that the bench was de-tagging the issue of the notice regime which was under challenge since there were already petitions which were also challenged by heterosexual couples. After lunch, a few seniors, including Raju Ramachandran and

Anand Grover, rushed to the court and asked the court to deal with it. Mr Ramachandran said that it would render the declaration—if we were to get that—illusory if the notice regime stayed in place. The Chief Justice countered it and said that since it applied to both heterosexual and homosexual couples, it was not prima facie discriminatory. Ramachandran replied that this was a constitutional issue which warranted a redressal from the court.

After lunch, Mehta resumed his arguments on why the reliance by the petitioners on *Ghaidan* was misplaced. He reiterated that a legislation could not be changed materially to make it constitutionally compatible, and that the court could not read something into the legislation that it was not intended to read. The Chief Justice chimed in that since the Indian Supreme Court had a wide power of interpretation, the tests which had to be applied to the statute had to be narrower. Bhat agreed and said that since there was a continuous interface between the two organs, it was up to the legislature to make it compatible. What the judges were hinting at through this statement was whether they could ask Parliament to enact a law. Mehta read between the lines and contended that the Supreme Court had never issued a writ of mandamus (issued a direction) to Parliament to enact a law, and it should not do so now.

The Solicitor General then mounted a siege on whether the right to marry itself was a fundamental right. He argued that the rights which were earlier enumerated by the Supreme Court were the right to love, cohabit, choose one's partner and choose one's sexual orientation. The Chief Justice said that one could not choose one's sexual orientation. Mehta reiterated that there was no fundamental right to seek recognition of either marriage or any other relationship by any name whatsoever. The Chief Justice again asked if there was any entitlement to recognition and Mehta shot back saying a lady in Gujarat married herself. How was the State to recognize it statutorily or otherwise? Notice how repeatedly the Solicitor General's arguments were reducing queer people to the butt of jokes by citing these examples. Yet again, this was an argument of alarm used as a joke. *'But Brutus is an honourable man.'*[2]

The Chief Justice then said that if the court accepted that there was a right to cohabit, then there was a corresponding duty on the State to ensure that these relationships get some recognition. Mehta responded by saying, or rather hinting, that it was not Indian tradition to recognize these relationships. The Chief Justice shot back saying that this was an impact of Victorian morality. Speaking about the profound nature of Indian culture, he said that what was imposed was a Victorian construct, and there were so many issues in it. Bhat agreed and said that there was a unique identity that was developed and inquired how the State wanted to handle this. Mehta said that he would speak to the relevant ministry and ask them to look into the issue. Pushing back on the earlier issue of recognition, he said that just because homosexuality was decriminalized, it did not mean that the State could be compelled to grant legal recognition. Kaul interjected and asked Mehta if there was no intended recognition nor regulation in case of a live-in relationship, could this be the case? Mehta replied defiantly that he *would* not assist the court in the removal of the problems that the community was facing without recognition, which he argued was not a fundamental right.

He then moved on to say that the arguments of the petitioners that the SMA was violative of Article 14 were unfounded. He argued that while the SMA applies when the government has created a mechanism for different classes though they are the same or vice versa, or the Act has no nexus with the object that it seeks to achieve, only then did it violate Article 14. He argued that the object of the SMA was only to allow marriage between heterosexual couples, and this was demonstrated by the language and architecture of the language. The object of the Act was to enable inter-caste and interfaith marriages, which it had achieved. He added that the State had to be slow to grant recognition to relationships, and since it was entering the personal arena, it could only be done when there was a legitimate State interest. He argued that even for heterosexual marriage, it was recognized only with the view that it should be regulated.

He reiterated that the choice to get a partner was a fundamental right; the right to recognition was not a fundamental right. He argued that unequals are not treated equally, and that the law imposed an obligation to exercise sexuality in private for homosexuals, and heterosexuals could express it publicly through the institution of marriage. He then said that the nature of the relationship and not sexual orientation was permitted by Article 14.

He then spoke about the Transgender Persons (Protection of Rights) Act. He told the bench that the way the word 'transgender' was defined was not how it was traditionally understood. He read the definition and argued that it covered all spectra and shades, broadly consisting of persons whose sex and gender did not match, and the Act was inclusive of persons who have undergone transformation surgery, intersex variations, and those who are gender-queer and other sociocultural identities. He argued that this included all persons within the LGBTQIA+ community. (Note: It does not.) There were gasps on our side, for this demonstrated a fundamental misunderstanding of gender and sexual

orientation. The Chief Justice read the room and stopped
Mehta. He said, 'Somebody who is gay is not someone whose
gender at birth does not match which gender he/she identifies
with—they are not transgenders. You may be right that this
definition covers all spectrums of transgenders, but gays and
lesbians are completely not covered.' Kaul chimed in and said
cisgender persons could not be transgender persons, but they
could be gays and lesbians. For once, Mehta acquiesced to
the bench and said that he could be wrong and was not an
expert on the issue. It was at this moment that his arguments
on the Trans Act applying to the entire community fell
flat. Mehta then argued that there was a historical amount
of stigma associated only with the transgender community:
Only to be countered by the Chief Justice who said that it was
evident from the debates which Mehta read out that there was
a considerable amount of stigma associated with the entire
community. Mehta knew where this was going and said that
the courts were not a forum for such debate. Kaul argued that
the debate was arising from what Mehta said, and he added
that Parliament could only have addressed the concerns and
reservations of the community. He then read out judgments
of cases from Thailand, Panama, Peru, Poland and the
Philippines and explained how the courts in each of these
countries denied legal recognition of LGBTQIA+ marriages.

Finally, in his last homophobic tirade, Mehta argued that
being gay or lesbian could be by birth, but it could also be
acquired, and this would have to be a consideration when the
legislature legislated. He argued that under the Constitution,
there were some derivative rights, and this was one such right.
He said that there was no need for a declaration, and that
there was no data to show that a majority of countries had
legalized non-heterosexual marriages. He argued that even a

friendship was an expression, but it could not be granted legal recognition.

The judges rose. Until now we were quite sure that that we were winning the case, especially since three judges—Kaul, Bhat and the Chief Justice—had pushed back on Mehta's veiled (and sometimes open) homophobia, especially in the post-lunch session. Little did we know that there would be a googly thrown at us the next morning, and the court would play along.

* * *

3 May: Day Seven

On the last date of the hearing, the judges had asked Mehta to confer with the ministries. Mehta came back on the next hearing date and said that he had spoken with various Union ministries. He proposed that there be a committee headed by the cabinet secretary to resolve the challenges that were faced by the queer community. There was vehement opposition by the petitioners' side on the ground that this issue had to be adjudicated upon. While we were open to sitting with the committee itself, we still hoped that there would be a declaration from the court. Abhishek Manu Singhvi and Menaka Guruswamy led the charge. Speaking first, Singhvi argued that whatever little could be achieved through administrative tweaking would be welcomed. However, there were larger issues which required legislative and judicial reforms which were way beyond the pay grade and domain of a cabinet secretary.

Mehta interfered by repeating his old argument and saying that this would lead to wider social issues. Classic conservative argument. Then he said if two old men were living together for companionship, they could not be said to be in a gay relationship. It was nobody's case that it could be. Guruswamy chimed in and argued that such an analogy missed the whole point. A queer relationship, she said, was an assertion of rights for two adults who were self-sufficient to live together in exercise of free will. She added that rights were a proactive, positive enactment that the law recognized, and the analogy missed the point. However, it was when Justice Kaul spoke up that we knew we had perhaps lost the case. He said that if the court agreed to a status of marriage or any other right then there were administrative and legislative changes required. He urged the petitioners to sit with the Union of India and see if a middle ground could be found. Even the Chief Justice, who was, in his opinions, the most proactive queer rights judge on the bench, kept on prodding the petitioners to sit with the government and work out some solution at the administrative level. He, however, argued that there would be three levels: First, the constitutional declaration of whether there was a fundamental right to marry; second, the legislative changes; and third, the administrative ones. What we were being told to do was take the bare minimum and be happy with it. This bare minimum was pink-washed in the proceedings as incremental changes which ought to have come by the judges. They believed that marriage was perhaps too quick a demand, and too radical.

Saurabh Kirpal chimed in and gave perhaps the most powerful oration—in my opinion—during the course of the hearings. I have refrained from quoting the exact words. He said, 'The vast majority of the young people I have spoken to have all said, "We want to get married." The parents of those young people have said, "We want to get married." My

Lords, we say, "We want to get married." "Why should we be second-class citizens?" There was a time we were criminals. Then we became third-class citizens. Now they're saying, "Be second-class citizens and then be content." That is not what the Constitution promised.' Justice Bhat then tried to tell the petitioners that they were perhaps asking for too much and too soon just years after decriminalization. He said that the community was aware of the history even better than the judges themselves. He urged the petitioners again to ask only for incremental reforms. His argument was that the movement for recognition and equality would continue. Having taken note of the arguments that the Solicitor General had made, the Chief Justice asked him to wrap up.

Mehta said he had three final propositions to make. First, he argued that there were a number of relationships that the State did not recognize because the state did not feel a compelling interest. Here, he argued, were multiple issues, like childbearing, maintenance, etc. Hence, the State must regulate marriages. Second, he argued that there were two pronouncements that the petitioners had relied upon: *Shakti Vahini* and *Shafin Jahan*. The latter was the famous Hadiya case. In both these cases, the Supreme Court had unequivocally held that the right to marry was a fundamental right. He argued that in these cases there was already a heterosexual marriage; and in the second, it was non-State actors who were objecting. In *Shakti Vahini*, the court was dealing with khap panchayats. Mehta argued that the institution of marriage could not be seen in the abstract. The Chief Justice clarified that this was not the argument, but the argument was that of non-discrimination. Mehta rejoined by saying that in both these cases, there were non-State actors who were acting to hinder the choice of a woman to marry the man she wished to get married to. He argued that there was an invasive, positive act by the State or non-State actor, despite the said marriage being recognized by law. Here, he said there was no marriage recognized by law and thus the petitioners' reliance on these judgments was unfounded.

Finally, the Solicitor General took the court through the judgment of Schalk and Kopf v. Austria.[3] Reading out a passage from the judgment, he placed reliance on the following extract: 'Man and women of marriageable age have the right to marry and to found a family according to the national laws governing the exercise of this right.' There were two issues, he said: The European convention reconsidered only a heterosexual marriage, and even that was subject to the domestic laws of each country. He showed that the convention clearly recognized that there was a Right to Marry under Article 12. Despite that recognition, the European Court of Human Rights had refused to locate the claims of same-sex marriage under Article 12.

Mehta finished his arguments. To say that sitting through these arguments was emotionally draining is an understatement. He was followed by the Attorney General of India, R. Venkataramani. With the benefit of hindsight, I think it was Venkataramani who made the briefest but perhaps the most balanced submissions. He stuck to the law and did not indulge in fear-mongering or causing moral panic as other lawyers had done. Much of his arguments were a rephrasing of what Mehta said on most points. Like Mehta, the Attorney General argued that the SMA was not discriminatory since it only allowed marriage for inter-caste and interfaith couples. He argued that since it only allowed marriages between heterosexual couples, it could not be under-inclusive, and to allow non-heterosexual couples to get married under this law would be to introduce an 'alien' intent into the law. He further argued,

The sole object of the Special Marriage Act being, facilitating and enabling [a] certain class of persons, desirous of accessing the institution of marriage. It intends to provide equal protection of the laws within the scope of Article 14 of the Constitution. Being so designed, it has no discriminatory content. As stated above, the Special Marriage Act is an enabling and facilitating legislation based on the common conception of marriage as a union of heterosexuals, the underlying premise in all laws relating to marriage. Marriage is a union of heterosexuals, being the universal conception of marriage. As such, the question of keeping in mind claims of other unions as marriage, and to accord them the same treatment, did not arise while enacting the Special Marriage Act.

Finally, he argued that the court could not rewrite the legislation as it would amount to violating a basic feature of the separation of powers. Within a few minutes, the Attorney General finished his arguments.

After the Attorney General, Senior Advocate Rakesh Dwivedi started his arguments after lunch for the State of MP. These arguments were perhaps the most acerbic, even more so than the Solicitor General's arguments. He began by saying that the demands raised in this petition were an omnibus demand raised by 'transgenders of seventy-two kinds, intersex genders, third-degree genders all'. He said the fundamental demand was ' . . . that 99 per cent of the transgenders could be accommodated as women or as per claim, whatever they put up. Yet, another demand, My Lord, was that this will not be sufficient to accommodate the third genders'. To say that Mr Dwivedi did not have a minimal understanding of gender and sexuality would not be wrong. Yet, here he was, opposing demands that he did not understand, making arguments rife with stereotypes. He said that any demand raised for marriage on the basis of the principles of autonomy, dignity and fraternity would affect the dignity of the heterosexual marriage. Quite strange considering the fact that marital rape is still criminalized in India, and that many women still find themselves in abusive and oppressive households and marriages. He then went on to say that when a man takes a woman as his wife, he does not take her as a spouse. He argued that the Supreme Court could not force a cultural revolution. He said *Obergefell* and *Fourie* could not be brought here and that the court should be averse to travel overseas. The Chief Justice was quick to counter it by saying that queerness was not imported.

Dwivedi then argued that this was not a cause that could be resolved by the court and that Parliament was the appropriate body to litigate the issue. He argued that since homosexuality was decriminalized five years ago, there was no rush to recognize marriages. He argued, 'All causes take time to succeed. All causes have martyrs.'

* * *

8 May: Day Eight

Dwivedi begin his argument the next day by posing a question: Is there a fundamental right to marry? The Chief Justice asked him if there was a fundamental right to marry for anyone. Dwivedi replied that the right to marry did not flow from any Article under Part 3 of the Constitution. His argument was that the institution of marriage flows from traditions, personal law and religion, and all of these only recognize heterosexual marriages. The institution of marriage, he argued, predated the

Constitution. This argument, in my submission, was flawed. The SMA is agnostic and secular. It does not flow from religion, personal law or tradition. That was its very purpose. Consider the right to education: which even in its institutional form has always existed, even prior to nation states as has the right to enter into contract. However, the same has not stopped the Supreme Court from recognizing these rights in their modern forms today. This is also a point that both the majority judgements miss.

He then went on to say that the population of India had grown only because people wanted to come together not for pleasure, but to reproduce. He argued that every religion said that procreation was a necessity for the purposes of marriage. Even adoption, Dwivedi posited, was only because of some heterosexual couple who had given up the child. He again urged the judges to not follow the *Obergefell* tradition. He said that marriage was the most sacred of all contracts. He argued that before giving a declaration the court had to deal with the following aspects:

1. What sort of recognition can be given to non-heterosexual relationships?
2. What is the form of such a recognition?
3. Can such a recognition be given under the existing law, or does it have to be incorporated into a separate law?
4. Can homosexual marriages be at par with heterosexual marriages?
5. If yes, to what extent can such a parity be given?
6. Can a blanket declaration be given in a single stroke, or does it have to be phased out?
7. If it has to be phased out, what should be the spacing of the phases?
8. What are the repercussions of gaining parity with heterosexual relationships?

9. What are the consequences of this parity?
10. Is the society ready to accept the recognition?

None of these arguments on societal recognition or consequences have ever been made before in issues of fundamental rights. The very purpose of these rights is that they are not contingent on popular or social morality, but only on constitutional morality. He argued that unless the court answered this question, any declaration would be too amorphous, and urged the court to not give such a declaration. Finally, he ended with two major issues: First, the SMA was enacted in 1954 when Section 377 was still on the statute books, and so when Parliament had codified inter-caste and interfaith marriages, it was lawful to discriminate. *Navtej* only decriminalized homosexuality a few years ago. Second, he argued that it was only a continuity of customs that these laws were discriminatory, and no amendment had occurred. He said that Parliament was the only body which was entitled to make such a legislation.

Dwivedi finished his arguments and was followed by Senior Advocate Kapil Sibal representing Jamiat, even though Muslim personal law was not a subject of the litigation. He started by saying that the declaration that the petitioners sought would limit the scope of Parliament, as there would be no scope for the debate. At the outset, Sibal misrepresented the argument of the petitioners by claiming that the petitioners wanted the declaration because we did not expect Parliament to act on the issue. To the contrary, we had provided the court with evidence of the fact that the issue of same-sex marriage had come up before Parliament, and Parliament in its wisdom had chosen not to act on it. So, this argument fell flat on its face.

His next argument was that this case was difference from *NALSA*, *Puttuswamy* and *Navtej*. Sibal said *NALSA* dealt with the sexual identity of transgenders. It did not. It dealt with gender identity. He then argued that the issues in this case were twofold: First, that there should be a sexual orientation that could be recognized by the Court, and second, whether such a union could be recognized by the State. Sibal argued that recognition should not flow from a declaration by the court but should instead be done by Parliament. He even took issue with recognizing the discrimination. He argued that recognition of marriage ought to be done by society and Parliament and that nothing stopped people from living together. Acceptance, he said, could not be gained through a legal or an administrative framework. I do not buy this argument. While there has been discrimination after *Navtej* also, the visibility of queer people has increased. That was a change rushed in by the court, and this case was yet another opportunity for the court to do it. Alas, it missed the opportunity. Yet, he ended on a sympathetic note by saying that the community must get something meaningful but it must fall short of marriage.

Sibal was followed by Arvind Datar, who had earlier appeared for the petitioners in *Navtej* and argued that Section 377 was unconstitutional. Yet, here he was on the other side, arguing against gay marriage. At the outset, like the other counsel before him, he argued that there was no fundamental right to marry. He argued that the passage in *Puttuswamy* which talked about the fundamental right to marry for queer persons was wrong because it was delivered before *Navtej*, and at the time homosexuality was still an offence. He argued that what was a fundamental right was a right to cohabit and form a union. Unlike counsels before him, however, his argument was that the law should be that which was enacted by Parliament and declared by the law. Under Article 141, the law declared by the Supreme Court is to be binding on all courts within the territory of India—and is thus law. When the Chief Justice queried whether his argument was that this right could not be recognized by the law, Datar replied in the negative and argued that it could be; however, it must be a future law only that can take this into account. It cannot be read into existing law, that is, the SMA. Finally, Datar argued that reading words into the SMA would amount to 'judicial retrofitting' by adding new parts or components to an old machine. What he meant was that the Act was enacted only for inter-caste and interfaith couples, and that the Supreme Court could not fit categories into the legislation which were not meant to originally fit into the scheme of the Act. He argued that there was a right to live in peace, but finding new rights and fitting them into old statutes would lead to dangerous situations.

I think both Datar and Sibal's arguments need to be dissected. They are based on a basic premise: While they both recognize that there is a right to cohabit and live in peace, that is a distant dream for many queer couples. The vulnerability and violence faced by them increases when the intersectionality of queer couples plays out. Marriage would give these couples legal protection which is otherwise not afforded to queer persons.

* * *

10 May: Day Nine

The next day had a flurry of counsel arguing before the Constitution bench led by the Chief Justice that was hearing the case seeking recognition of marriage and adoption by numerous queer couples. As the days passed, the bench seemed to be on edge. They were guillotining the time sought by counsel for arguments, and perhaps for the right reasons. Five judges had heard the case over nine days, and there were still arguments which had to be made in rejoinder. Our system of arguments often involves making long-winded submissions, and saying in a thousand words what can be said in ten. The fact that this was one of the first cases of vital importance that was being live-streamed didn't help the grandstanding of lawyers.

The day began with Senior Advocate and Additional Solicitor General Aishwarya Bhati appearing for the National Commission for Protection of Child Rights (NCPCR). She told the court that while the application was filed on behalf of the NCPCR, the Ministry of Women and Child Development and the Central Adoption Regulatory Authority (CARA) had also provided her with inputs. Her primary argument was opposing adoptions by queer persons.

She argued that the basic structure of a marriage is between a man and a woman. Secondly, she argued that gender fluidity was impermissible when cisgender was the core of the legislation. This argument was not buttressed with any example, or statutory provision or with evidence that supported this claim. There is a well-settled law passed which recognizes the right to self-determination of gender in *NALSA*. Though the Trans Act itself does not recognize non-binary genders and instead puts them under a common 'T' marker under S. 6 Trans ID Cards, it is to that extent, in my opinion, unconstitutional. Bhati further argued that allowing gender fluidity would compromise women's equality. These are old arguments which have been used by Trans Exclusionary Radical Feminists and have been debunked a thousand times. I do not wish to carry coals to Newcastle. Notably, these arguments have been imported into India by an overenthusiastic group of people calling themselves women's rights activists with little or no understanding of how patriarchy harms both cisgender and transgender women. This is dangerous and shows that the government is playing an active in building an anti-gender movement for which queer rights activists ought to be prepared.

At the heart of every case of adoption or case of custody, she argued, was the welfare of the child, which was paramount and sacrosanct. She argued that there was a legitimate interest of the State in protecting the 'ideal mode of child-rearing', that children born naturally to heterosexual couples should be raised by heterosexual couples. There are no competing interests here, she said, pitting the rights of the child against the right of queer persons to adopt. There was no argument made to this effect by the petitioners. Our argument on the issue of discrimination was that queer persons should be allowed to adopt as couples when heterosexual couples could do so. It was nobody's case that the rights of the child ought to be pitted against the right of queer persons to adopt.

She argued then that the recognition of marriage could not be an understatement, and that the State treats couples differently since both the mother and the father play a vital role in the growth and development of a child. Marriage, she said, was not a factory for childbearing, but to encourage men and women to create a generation in the right environment. Building upon the concept of *parens patriae*, or the role of the State as a guardian of the child, she argued, the Union had taken multiple steps to ensure that children are brought up by caring and nurturing families. Biological birth, she said, was the norm and adoption an exception.

At this point, Justice Bhat intervened and said that the State allows adoptions by single parents, whether males or females, but the moment they enter into a same-sex or live-in relationship, the State prohibits them from adopting. The Chief Justice added that the moment people entered into a live-in relationship they could not even adopt as a single parent. Justice Kaul asked that if there was an adoption first, and then a future live-in relationship, then that could not be a disqualification. Bhati placed extensive reliance on the CARA guidelines and said that if a couple wanted to adopt now, they would have to be heterosexual.

Justice Narsimha, who had been virtually silent, spoke up at this point. He said that the moment a heterosexual marital relationship is entered into, the husband becomes an adoptive father and the woman the adoptive mother. As a result, the child becomes the heir in the event of the death of both. If a single parent enters into a same-sex relationship, the adoptive child continues to remain the adoptive child to the same parent and no more. In the event of disruption of the family, Narsimha said, like in cases of divorce, the relationship of an adoptive child continues. Bhat said that it was in the interest of the child that there should be at least one parent who was responsible for the child.

Bhati then argued that it was obvious that in a civilized society the importance of child welfare could not be overemphasized because the welfare of the entire community, its growth and development depended on the health and well-being of children. What followed next was an interesting discussion on the number of couples who could be prospective parents. Bhati confirmed that there were 1500 parents who were available. Bhat showed great concern at this.

Finally, Bhati argued that altering the text of the SMA would have a negative impact on children.

Bhati was followed by Maninder Singh, a senior advocate, who argued that by virtue of interpretation, it was not possible for the court to recognize same-sex marriage. Showing the judgments of various courts, he argued that unlike other courts, there was no law like the Defence of Marriage Act in the United States which put a bar on same-sex marriage which could be struck down. The second leg of his argument was that an ability to procreate was a condition under Section 4 of the SMA and the inability to procreate was a ground for divorce.

He argued that under all personal laws, marriage was based on the moral and legal equality of the spouses. He also argued that in terms of access to the ancillary rights, the institution of marriage, was distinct from the benefits which arose from the benefits arising out of it. He said that the difficulty or even a perceived hardship involved in obtaining the benefit of a means of legal challenge did not justify bypassing a basic law.

He was followed by Atmaram Nadkarni who appeared for the Akhil Bharatiya Sant Samiti. His submissions had two prongs: First, that marriage in Indian society is the creation of an institution. For Hindus, it is a sacrament, while for Muslims, it is a contract. He argued that the very concept of same-sex marriage was virtually an attack on the institution of marriage as it was traditionally known in India. He argued that merely because the right to privacy had been recognized, it did not necessarily mean that the right to marriage was also recognized. He, however, argued that the court could recognize a civil union and a declaration that queer people should and would not be harassed, but he argued that India had not reached a level where the institution of marriage could be permitted at this stage, alluding to Roscoe Pound's concept of social engineering. I often hear these arguments, and the answer to them is simple. Under international law, there are two genera of rights: Civil and political rights, which have to be immediately enforced, and cultural, economic and social rights, which are to be progressively realized.

Though the rights were initially differentiated into two categories, viz, civil and political rights and economic, social and cultural rights on account of the cold war tensions and the difference between the importance given by the West to civil and political rights, while the East favoured economic, social and cultural rights. Be that as it may, there is now broad consensus that the rights are now interlinked and the differentiation between the two is erased. Notably, later treaties such as the Convention on the rights of the Child and the Convention on persons with disabilities integrate both categories of rights into a single treaty. However, since economic, cultural and social rights require higher investment by the nation states, they are said to be progressively realizable. Civil and Political rights on the other hand, simply require the State to not interfere with liberties of citizens.[4]

Marriage is a civil and political right and thus immediately enforceable. The benefits arising out of marriage, however, fall within the latter category and can be progressively realized as the march for equality continues.

Nadkarni was followed by Manisha Lavkumar, who was appearing on behalf of the state of Gujarat. She argued that there was a need for a wider consultative process and comprehensive deliberation before same-sex marriage could be recognized. She argued that the case before the court was not a case of exclusion or prohibition, but a case of non-inclusion in a targeted legislation, enacted with special aims and objects. Thus, she said, the SMA was not discriminatory.

Her next argument was that marriage as a socially recognized institution and the foundation of the Indian family unit was at the core of the hearing. She argued that the State's interest in allowing only heterosexual marriages was necessary to preserve social order, ensure progression of society in a legitimate manner and regulate matrimonial conduct. Marriage was sanctified—the principle of sanctification, she argued, lies in the fact that the institution of marriage predated any legislation, then legislation recognized the institution, and then related it to the bringing up of children. She said that the regulation of private lives did not end at marriage; it also dictated parties enter and exit the marriage through a gamut of laws. She argued that any declaration issued by the court would have ramifications on matrimonial laws and other ancillary laws. She argued that without proper deliberations, there would be chaos. She contended that the petitioner's apprehensions that Parliament would not look into it were misconceived. She argued that approaching the court was a circuitous route to get Parliament to look into the matter.

Then she said that the first endeavour of the petitioners was to read into the SMA. When the petitioners realized that the demands were not fitting into the structure of the SMA, they now sought a declaration apart from the SMA, which would have even more serious ramifications. She argued that such a declaration would foreclose the rights of society and hamper genuine, organic and sustainable change in society. She argued that this was reflective of the democratic ethos of the working of the Constitution. Finally, she said that this was not a case of mere declaration but one where the court ought to examine the resultant ramifications of the declaration.

Lavkumar was followed by Sai Deepak, who virtually yelled his submissions at the bench. What he lacked in substance he made up with the conviction with which he made them. He represented a women's organization. He posed a question to the bench: If the Constitution is liberal, and it constitutes a liberal democracy, did social conservatism have no place? The answer to this is no. The Constitution is liberal and thus our governing philosophy has to be liberal. Personally, people are free to have their beliefs, but interpersonal relations have to be governed by a liberal philosophy. He argued that the petitioners had a cause; they did not have a case. A lot of us on the petitioners' side giggled when this happened. Little did we know that this was ultimately what the court would decide. He argued that the question of marriage equality was based on the legislative prerogative, but also that society must have a right to participate. He argued that since Section 21 of the SMA had a bearing on personal laws, society had a right to participate.

He then sought to distinguish the NALSA judgment and argued that it must be read in context, where the issue was limited to the recognition of a third gender, and that it should not be stretched beyond that. To extrapolate the findings therein would amount to reading a judgment for what it is not, he argued. Justice Bhat, who had by now had enough of Sai Deepak's tone and tenor, said, 'I think we perhaps are aware of how to read this judgment. Please, we don't need to be taught.' Sai Deepak was quick to apologize. He then argued that reading *NALSA* would lead to distinctions between the judges on gender identity and sexual orientation. He argued that the NALSA judgment demonstrated how narrow language when expanded through judicial interpretation leads to a lot of principles.

He was followed by M.R. Shamshad, who argued that even in the statutory regime of laws, there was ample space for undefined customs and practices of every community and those who follow religious beliefs have been made a part of the statute. Ultimately, he said, the court does not know what custom is and it needs to be proved on a case-to-case basis. He further argued that same-sex marriages would not be recognized by the personal laws of some communities.

After a few counsels who made brief submissions, which were broadly reiterations of the previous arguments, Sasmit Patra, representing two organizations, began his arguments. They were based on two issues: The capacity of Parliament, and the role of the judiciary in policy framing. Arguing that the role of polity was crucial, he said that the court could not ignore the impact on public policy. He argued that Parliament had the capacity to deal with issues arising in this matter which had wide ramifications. He further argued that when the court gives a declaration, there is an effective declaration of the law.

As a result, he said, there were public policy precepts, and thus the implementation of such a declaration would be difficult.

Atulesh Kumar, who argued next, drew the attention of the court that the issue was not on personal law but only the SMA. He argued that the SMA was not a legislation that could be looked at in isolation—it affected personal laws also.

Multiple counsels argued briefly then. Most of those arguments were a repetition of the ones that were already advanced before. Someone said that bisexuality and pansexuality led to bigamy and cheating; yet another counsel argued that since there was no awareness, there ought to be a law first, and only then could marriage equality be allowed. None of these arguments merit any attention. One counsel, Anson Thomas, appearing virtually, also sought the recusal of the Chief Justice. His application was of course rejected. Not only that, the Solicitor General also vehemently opposed the application for recusal.

The Solicitor General had opened the arguments for the respondents; he also ended them. He opposed the submissions made by the counsel on the side of the respondents that even something less than marriage could be given. This, he said was the first issue that he was drawing the attention of the court to. The second issue, he said, was the case of the bakers and pastors in the United States who refused to provide their services to gay couples for their weddings.[5] Mehta asked if a declaration were to be given, would a priest have to follow it? Bhat said that it would breach his fundamental right to faith and that the kind, form and contours of this declaration—if the court issued it—would recognize the state of affairs. Mehta argued that a declaration would not have the wherewithal to foresee and comprehend the effect of the declaration and would not be able to deal with the fallout.

The Chief Justice then asked if Mehta's argument was that the declaration by the court would pre-empt the legislature from considering the issue. Mehta answered in the negative. He said that the legislature could do something but argued that a declaration by the court would put a stop to dissent. He argued that closing debates would lose minds. Finally, he placed forward letters written by the governments of Manipur, Andhra Pradesh, Uttar Pradesh, Maharashtra, Assam, Sikkim and Rajasthan, which had all opposed the grant of marriage equality.

There were some trite issues which came up: Gendered laws, patriarchy, feminism and queering legislation, which came up in the arguments of multiple counsel. But these differences were not that vast or that irreconcilable. Bhati, in her arguments, raised gender-critical feminism and trans-exclusionary feminism and this had its origins in the current state of polity where anything that is thought to have originated in the West is decried. People in India seem to be fine with trans people begging on the streets or doing sex work, but when they attain some form of agency, trans-ness suddenly becomes a Western import. Fallacious slippery-slope arguments and a minimal understanding of gender identity and sexual orientation shone through. Sitting through them took a huge mental and emotional toll on me.

Note here that the bench sought to not deal with the issue of the notice regime, and the matter was mentioned again. It was dealt with in detail in the written submissions, and the opening arguments, and the rejoinder, as you will see in the next chapter. Yet, not once did the bench tell us that they would not decide the issue.

Finally, a caveat. Like I said at the end of the last chapter, the arguments and analysis of this chapter are based both on revisiting recordings, transcripts and my own daily notes from the court. The critique here is not directed at the counsel, who are holding a brief, but at the arguments themselves.

Chapter 6

The Return Fire

*Veil after veil of thin dusky gauze is lifted, and by degrees the
forms and colours of things are restored to them, and we watch
the dawn remaking the world in its antique pattern.*
—Oscar Wilde, *The Picture of Dorian Gray*[1]

In our legal system, a case is opened by the petitioners.
Then there is a reply by the respondents, and finally, the
petitioners are allowed to respond to the arguments of the
respondents. These are called the arguments in rejoinder.
After Mehta had finished his arguments on day nine, Dr
Singhvi opened the rejoinder arguments and took up a
major chunk of the following day, and the rest of the counsel
finished it over the remainder of the day. At the outset, the
senior counsel asked the court that it should exercise the
power it had to its maximum and grant the right to marry.
He said that the petitioners could not wait until Parliament
drafted a law to recognize non-heterosexual marriage. He
argued that the court would be well within its powers to
recognize the discriminatory language of the SMA and read
the words 'husband' and 'wife' as 'spouse'. He drew parallels
with the arguments made by the petitioners in *Navtej*.

There was significant resistance here from both Justices Bhat and Kohli. Their argument seemed to be that this was not an ordinary prayer for striking down a legislation as would be the usual course but one that asked the court to read into the statute. Singhvi said that all that the petitioners were asking the court was to strike down the exclusion of persons belonging to the LBGTQIA+ community by reading the statute in a gender-neutral fashion. He also opposed the argument that the court would be entering the realm of judicial legislation by reading the Act in a way that would encase a hitherto excluded class of citizens. He argued that the petitioners were seeking their equality in its full strength. To give them an institution of a civil union or something less than marriage reinforced the 'separate but equal doctrine'. He did this by putting in his written submissions the powerful picture of six-year-old Ruby Bridges, the first African-American girl to go to William Frantz Elementary School in New Orleans in November 1960. To escape the protesting crowds, she had to be escorted by federal marshals. Much later in life, she would go on to say, 'I now know that experience comes to us for a purpose, and if we follow the guidance of the spirit within us, we will probably find that the purpose is a good one.'

Finally, in the last leg of his arguments, Singhvi urged the bench to reject what he called the 'scare arguments' which were advanced by the Union. He argued that if the court wanted, it could stay away from interpreting personal laws. The limited issue, he said, was the issue of succession for Hindus, Buddhists, Sikhs and Jains which fell in the SMA. Even that could be avoided, he said, if the bench read the word 'spouse' into the Hindu Succession Act and the Indian Succession Act. The bench did not agree. Justice Bhat said that this would amount to entering the domain of personal laws. But here is the thing, the issue of personal laws was under challenge. The bench had chosen not to act on it. Perhaps in a hurry or demonstrating a lack of foresight about Section 21A of the SMA, the bench had no option but to enter into the realm of personal laws. This would have meant that Hindu queer couples would have continued to be governed by the Hindu law in matters of succession. All he had proposed was that either the court let the SMA be as it is, or reinterpret it, or find out a third and new policy solution. The first was based on incremental rights as they accrue in common law with each judgment, the second was to read the SMA in a way that would make it compliant with the Constitution, and the final one was what the court had done earlier in *Vishaka* or the case concerning the process of selection of Election Commissioner's where they had virtually created a new law which would hold the field until Parliament enacted a new law. These were not novel propositions. There was distinct scorn from the bench. When Singhvi presented his workability model, again there was a caustic remark by one of the judges from the bench: 'We are not here to write blog articles, we have to deliver a workable judgment,' they said. This was a below-the-belt attack on one of the counsels assisting Singhvi.

After this exchange, I think most of us realized that the bench would not grant us the right to marry under the SMA. But we had still hoped that they would recognize a fundamental right to marry. Reading the room, Mukul Rohatgi stood up and said that even if the bench did not want to recognize marriage equality under the SMA, it could do so by drafting an affidavit executed and signed by both parties and recognize it as a valid registration under the SMA. I am of the opinion that this undercut our case to a certain extent. However, even in this suggestion, Rohatgi had argued that marriage equality must be recognized.

Section 18 of the Registration Act, which allows for certain documents to be registered at the option of the parties, reads as follows:

Any of the following documents may be registered under this Act, namely:

a. Instruments (other than instruments of gift and wills) which purport or operate to create, declare, assign, limit or extinguish, whether in present or in future, any right, title or interest, whether vested or contingent, of a value less than one hundred rupees, to or in immovable property;

b. instruments acknowledging the receipt or payment of any consideration on account of the creation, declaration, assignment, limitation or extinction of any such right, title or interest;

c. leases of immovable property for any term not exceeding one year, and leases exempted under Section 17;

[1][(cc) instruments transferring or assigning any decree or order of a court or any award when such decree or order or award purports or operates to create, declare, assign, limit or extinguish, whether in present or in future, any right, title or interest, whether vested or contingent, of a value less than one hundred rupees, to or in immovable property;

d. instruments (other than wills) which purport or operate to create, declare, assign, limit or extinguish any right, title or interest to or in movable property;

e. wills; and

f. all other documents not required by Section 17 to be registered.

With that, the judges rose for the day. There was a final day of arguments left before the lengthy battle was over.

* * *

10 May: Day Nine

Continuing his arguments from the previous day, Senior Advocate Dr Abhishek Manu Singhvi who was appearing on behalf of the petitioners continued his arguments in rejoinder on the final day. At the outset, he showed the bench the areas of challenge and the challenges in his petition. His argument was that the challenge in the petitions was only to the provisions which were exclusionary to queer couples and not the entire Act. As a result, there were no special protections which were afforded under the law which would be affected. He made it clear that gendered laws should continue, including special laws relating to rape and sexual assault. However, he called non-binary and intersex people a 'theoretical category'. I was in court. I was not a theoretical category. The last part sullied what was otherwise a stellar argument for me. He reiterated that his argument was seeking nothing more than a Constitution-compliant reading of the SMA. Then he wrapped up his arguments.

Singhvi was followed by Senior Advocate Raju Ramachandran. He argued that there would be consequences if the court merely left it to the legislature to enact the law on marriage. He demonstrated this through three issues: Triple talaq, where the legislature had gone beyond the diktat of the court and criminalized it; the data protection law, where there was no law despite there being a right to privacy, which was recognized; and finally, transgender rights, where a law was passed four years after the judgment recognized the rights of transgender persons. He said these issues had enjoyed popularity and a consensus in the legislative assembly. However, the queer community was an 'unpopular minority' across communities and political parties.

The Chief Justice said that the court could not decide an issue based on how Parliament would respond. He said that the court had to fulfil its duty as the sentinel on the qui vive, and 'walk the full mile and not stop at [a] constitutional declaration'. Ramachandran reiterated and argued at length that the notice regime ought to be struck down, or the court should deal with a protocol under the SMA or by recognizing constitutional rights. Without this, he argued, there would be no protection for vulnerable couples, and any relief that was granted would be rendered illusory. Finally, Ramachandran said that while the court was dealing with reading the SMA in a Constitution-compliant manner, it should keep in mind three things:

1. First, the provisions affording special provision to the wife will stand as they are and are not affected by the interpretation in a queer-inclusive manner.
2. Second, the argument that this would also affect penal laws which affect women was misplaced since the penal laws were not a subject matter of challenge.
3. Finally, the mandate of the litigation, as set by the court, was such that religious laws are not interfered with.

Finally, he argued that the test of constitutionality should only be that the test is not whether the tradition of marriage under religious law should be touched, but whether such a reading was discriminatory.

Ramachandran was followed by Senior Advocate K.V. Viswanathan (as he then was). He argued that there was a positive obligation on the state to recognize that there was a right to marry, and as a result, there was also a corresponding duty on the Union to recognize that non-heterosexual marriages are recognized in a manner that is non-discriminatory. Even if such a recognition was a privilege, there cannot be any discrimination. The core of his argument in rejoinder was that when discrimination is based on an innate or a core trait—what Dr Singhvi had called 'ascriptive' characteristic— he argued that there was an obligation on the State to not discriminate. Since he was representing Zainab Patel, he also argued that the lack of workability was not enough justification to discriminate. Finally, he said that there was full entitlement to the heterosexual community to marry as well as the protection of their rights on divorce, and queer persons should not be deprived of their right to live freely.

Senior Advocate Geeta Luthra appeared next. Her argument was essential for much of it focused on the importance of the prevalence of constitutional morality over the social ethos that the respondent had relied on. She argued that traditions which were not in tune with the philosophy and principles of the Constitution could not be relied on. In view of constitutional comity, she argued that constitutional morality ought to be placed above ephemeral and vague social norms. Finally, she argued that not only should the court read into the SMA for non-heterosexual couples, but it should also recognize the right to marry and the right to have a family.

Senior Advocate Anand Grover appeared next. Over the few weeks since we had finished arguments, we had discussed that the issue of stigma that was brought up must be dealt with. Grover argued that the stigma which was attached by the

British morality to non-heterosexual relationships continued with the denial of the right to marry. He argued that there are grave consequences for the queer community if they were denied the right to marry, and if the court denies that right or does not recognize it, the situation would worsen. This prophecy has come true after the verdict. From judges calling queer people 'immoral', to the denial of performing the final rights for a partner who is disowned by their family, the community is much worse off after the verdict. Grover argued that the argument of no stigma was fallacious because to this date the respondents were still to come to terms with queer persons. Our sexualities are no different, he thundered. Placing reliance on the right to associate and the right to form intimate associations under Article 19(1)(c) of the Constitution, he argued that the fundamental right to marry was manifest in the Constitution.

Grover also relied on international law, and specifically the Convention on the Elimination of All Forms of Discrimination against Women (CEDAW) to argue that India has an obligation to respect, fulfil and protect fundamental rights. He also argued *that under CEDAW, which India had signed and ratified, the State was bound to remove* ' . . . *any distinction, exclusion or restriction made on the basis of sex which has the effect or purpose of impairing or nullifying the recognition, enjoyment or exercise by women, irrespective of their marital status, on a basis of equality of men and women, of human rights and fundamental freedoms in the political, economic, social, cultural, civil or any other field.*'[2] Finally, Grover read out paragraphs from the poem 'The Love that Dares to Speak Its Name' by James Kirkup.[3]

Senior Advocate Jayna Kothari then followed. Going back to the debates of Parliament, she argued that at the core of the SMA was the shift in the very conception of marriage.

She argued that what had initially been a sacrament was now an instrument of freedom and choice to facilitate inter-caste and interfaith marriages. She argued that the marriages of queer persons fall within this conception, and all that the petitioners sought was that the court interpret the SMA with the real intent behind the enactment of the legislation and give it a purposive interpretation.

Senior Advocate Dr Menaka Guruswamy argued next. Guruswamy was appearing on behalf of the DCPCR. Her arguments were focused on adoption by queer persons. Citing and relying on multiple studies, as also the decisions of various constitutional and Supreme Courts around the world, she made a passionate case for marriage equality for queer parents. She argued that there were numerous meta-studies around the world which had demonstrated that not only was there no adverse effect of parenting by queer and transgender persons, but the kids brought up by them also outperformed those raised by heterosexual persons in terms of emotional and psychological development. Guruswamy also pointed out studies that demonstrated that children brought up by queer persons had better economic outcomes than those who were not. She argued that since sexuality develops at a young age, the denial of rights also affects the younger generation of LGBTQ persons psychologically. Finally, she showed a report by the Indian Psychiatrist Society which she said was the largest society of mental health professionals in India consisting of 7000 psychiatrists that explicitly said that discrimination against the LGBTQIA++ community leads to mental-health issues. She argued that this could only be done by sensitizing and raising awareness about queer rights.

Saurabh Kirpal was one of the last lawyers to flank the arguments in this case. He argued that a declaration in a vacuum with no practical impact would be a futile exercise. Hence, he prayed that the court should issue a declaration under Section 4 of the SMA which would ensure that the declaration precipitates into actual rights. He argued that such declarations would not only not render the SMA unworkable, it would also not cause violence to the language of the SMA. He argued that it was not the whole Act that was to be reinterpreted but only sub-sections (c) and (d). Even if a solution was potentially unworkable, he said, it was still better than nothing. He said that the issues could be dealt with by the courts as and when they arose and the claim of unworkability could not be used as a defence to constitutional validity so as to find a way around ensuring fundamental rights.

Arundhati Katju finished up the submissions in rejoinder. Drawing an analogy with the evolution of trans rights after *NALSA*, her argument was that since the pronouncement of the declaration would be law under Article 141, she argued that it would bind Parliament and the judiciary, and lead to a gradual evolution of rights. She said that the recognition and declaration of transgender persons as a 'third gender', she pointed to various schemes in states and the Union which were meant to protect transgender persons. Extending the argument of Kirpal, she said that the right to marry must translate into precipitative outcomes for the day-to-day life of queer persons and that could only be done by recognizing the right to marry under the SMA. Finally, she said the right to marry was located in a variety of fundamental rights, including Articles 14, 15, 19 and 21, and that the court ought to recognize the right to marry by conferring on queer persons the status of marriage.

With this, the marathon hearings came to an end. Little did we know what the outcome would be, for we were joyous at the end of the hearings. But here, the ending of this case and the pronouncement of the judgment was the initiation of a new fight.

What followed was an excruciating wait. But things were calm. There was some gossip going around, as it always does, about which way the case would go but one did not pay attention to it. Little did I know that this was the calm before the storm, and that all hell would break loose on queer people come October.

But a few reflections are apposite at this juncture: the case started with a few personal laws and the special marriage act being challenged. Then came petitions like Zainab Patel's petition which sought marriage equality 'under all laws'. This was followed by Rituparnah Borah's petition seeking recognition of 'natal families'. Some counsel like Rohatgi seemed to give up the fight halfway and argued that a mere affidavit should suffice which would be registered. It ended up being a hotch-potch which, if my math is right, came down to 9-10 different outcomes within the Special Marriage Act. All solutions came through with different counsel using diverse schools of jurisprudence which led to confusion amongst the judges, as was evident during the hearings. This, of course, calls for a more consultative and collaborative approach to a rights-based litigation that affects the community at large.

Chapter 7

Excluded but Not Condemned:
The Judgment and the Way Ahead

In forming a marital union, two people become something greater
than once they were. As some of the petitioners in these cases
demonstrate, marriage embodies a love that may endure even past
death . . . Their hope is not to be condemned to live in loneliness,
excluded from one of civilization's oldest institutions. They ask
for equal dignity in the eyes of the law. The Constitution
grants them that right.
—Obergefell v. Hodges, 576 US 644

On the evening of the judgment, Saurabh Kirpal invited a
few of us to his house. I have been the subject of Saurabh and
his partner Nico's kindness, generosity and warmth despite
knowing them less than a year. They have been there for me
through the highs and the lows. To say we were dejected was
an understatement. I am not sure about the others but I had
broken down into tears multiple times throughout that day.
Saurabh, forever the optimist, asked us to lick our wounds,
start fighting back and start preparing and drafting our
reviews which had to be filed in the next thirty days. He said,
'The court has let us down, but we cannot let the community

down.' I wrote these words in my journal that day, and they have stayed with me.

Overall, the court's judgment and opinions had dealt with two issues from the range argued before it: The right to marry and the right to adopt. Both these claims were rejected. While the right to marry was rejected by all five judges, the right to adopt was allowed by two judges and disallowed by three.

On the issue of whether there was a fundamental right to marry, four judges said no, while Justice Kaul's opinion was silent on the issue. Justice Chandrachud said that allowing such a right to marry would compel the State to create a new institution when it has chosen not to create it. This argument was fallacious because we were not seeking the creation of a new institution but merely that those who wanted to be allowed into the institution of marriage as created by the SMA be allowed to do that. Justices Bhat and Kohli held that marriage existed independently of the State, and that the court could not compel the State to create a legal status. Justice Narsimha held that this was a fundamental freedom, but not a fundamental right. Note here that there is no definition of status or an institution. However, the court held that transgender persons in heterosexual marriages were allowed to marry their partner, according to the Chief Justice and Justice Bhat. Simply put, this means that trans men can marry trans women or cis women, and trans women can marry trans men or cis men. This followed the celebrated judgment by the Madras High Court in Arunkumar's case[1] and gave it the judicial imprimatur of the Constitution bench and was perhaps the only good thing to come out of this litigation. What happens to those of us who are non-binary, gender-queer or agender? The court does not deal with it—perhaps we are too much of a 'minuscule minority' for the court to even think about us.

The Chief Justice rejected the claim that queerness was either urban or elite. After elucidating the background of the petitioners before the court, he notes,

> The respondents, including the Union of India, have contended that homosexuality and queer gender identities or transgenderism are predominantly present in urban areas and amongst the elite sections of society. They assert that variations in gender and sexual identity are largely unknown to rural India and amongst the working classes. Nothing could be further from the truth. While they may not use the words "homosexuality," 'queer', lesbian', 'gay' or any other term which populates the lexicon of English-speaking persons, they enter into unions with persons of the same sex as them or with gender queer persons; these unions are often long-lasting, and the couple performs a marriage ceremony. The incidence of queerness amongst the rural and working-class communities has been documented in academic scholarship as well as newspaper reports.To imagine queer persons as existing only in urban and affluent spaces is to erase them even as they exist in other parts of the country. It would also be a mistake to conflate the 'urban' with the 'elite'. This renders invisible large segments of the population who live in urban spaces but are poor or otherwise marginalized. Urban centres are themselves geographically and socially divided along the lines of class, religion, and caste and not all those who live in cities can be termed elite merely by virtue of their residence in cities.

On the issue of whether the court had the power to declare that there was a right to marry, four judges (save for Justice Kaul whose opinion is silent on the issue) held that they could not. Justice Chandrachud's opinion said that other entitlements, if not recognized, would render the right to relationship otiose, but that it was for the State to recognize that, and the court could not. Justice Bhat took a different line of argument and held that this was venturing too much into the domain of the legislature. This is the same court which had, out of thin air, created a law on various issues: Sexual harassment in *Vishaka*,[2] appointment of the Election Commission in *Anoop Baranwal*,[3] and even on divorce, where it created a new ground of divorce when none existed in *Shilpa Sailesh*.[4]

Once the court had dealt with the fundamental jurisprudence around rights, it moved on to the SMA, where it focused on three issues: First, on the gender-neutral interpretation of the SMA to read the words 'husband' or 'wife' as 'spouse'; second, on the question of whether a right to marry can be read into the SMA to save it from unconstitutionality; and finally, on whether the SMA is unconstitutional for not including queer couples within its ambit.

The first and second issues are intertwined with each other because the prayer was that if the constitutional validity of the SMA is suspect, then the court should either declare it to be void or read it down by deleting phrases judicially from the statute or add phrases to it through judicial interpretation. So I will deal with them together. None of these things were unknown to law and have been done widely by both our court and courts around the world. For example, in *Navtej*, the court read down Section 377 to include, from its ambit, unnatural intercourse between consenting adults. On the issue of reading the SMA in a gender-neutral fashion, the court was divided on the means, but the end was the same, namely that the SMA cannot be interpreted in a gender-neutral fashion. Chief Justice Chandrachud said,

If the SMA is held void for excluding same-sex couples, it would take India back to the pre-Independence era where two persons of different religions and caste were unable to celebrate love in the form of marriage. Such a judicial verdict would not only have the effect of taking the nation back to the era when it was clothed in social inequality and religious intolerance but would also push the Article 13 of the Constitution courts to choose between eradicating one form of discrimination and prejudice at the cost of permitting another. If this court takes the second approach and reads words into the provisions of the SMA and provisions of other allied laws such as the ISA [Indian Succession Act] and HSA [Hindu Succession Act], it would in effect be entering into the realm of the legislature.

Now this was an extremist view. The court could have easily said that it is unconstitutional insofar as it allows only heterosexual marriage. To say that striking down the SMA would take us back into 'the era when it was clothed in social inequality and religious intolerance' is what happened when the court refused the fundamental right to marry for queer couples. By reducing it to the level of a statutory right, what the court was saying was that such a right was subject to the whims and fancies of the legislature, and not a constitutional guarantee. The right was something that Parliament giveth, and Parliament taketh away. When a right is protected as a fundamental right, the level of protection is higher, because you can directly approach the high court or the Supreme Court for redress. What happens now when interfaith and inter-caste couples are harassed by State and non-State actors? What happens when laws that are couched as supposedly anti-conversion laws or 'love jihad' laws are passed by state legislature which virtually prohibit interfaith marriages without risking safety and privacy? The court has now allowed the legislature to determine who can marry and how they can marry. In all of these issues, if the court were to adjudicate as it did in this petition, it would uphold such laws. Would that not toss us into 'the era when it was clothed in social inequality and religious intolerance'? The answer, my friend, is blowin' in the wind.

Justice Bhat's opinion concurred with the Chief Justice on this issue. He held that the exclusion of non-heterosexual relationships was not fatal to the constitutionality of the SMA, and that such discrimination was permissible. Speaking further on the issue of a gender-neutral interpretation of the SMA, he held,

> Gender-neutral interpretation, much like many seemingly progressive aspirations, may not really be equitable at times and can result in women being exposed to unintended vulnerability, especially when genuine attempts are made to achieve a balance, in a social order that traditionally was tipped in favour of cis-heterosexual men . . . Gender-neutral interpretation of existing laws, therefore, would complicate an already exhausting path to justice for women and leave room for the perpetrator to victimize them. A law is not merely meant to look good on paper; but is an effective tool to remedy a perceived injustice, addressed after due evaluation about its necessity. A law which was consciously created and fought for by women cannot, therefore, by an interpretive sleight be diluted.

Justice Narsimha agreed with Justice Bhat on this issue. This is a classic argument of moral panic: Queer rights are not meant to oppose the rights of women, nor are they in conflict with women's rights. Rather, they both serve the same end: To smash patriarchy. We have seen this often in the bathroom debates, or in the participation of transgender persons in sports. This is seemingly done to protect women from men. As bioessentialism rears its debate in the issues of trans rights in India, as it has done in this case, its transmutation in the broader queer rights debate was only a logical sequitur. So, much of the work of queer and trans activists and advocates has been positioned towards interrogating and undoing assumptions that cis hetero-patriarchy conditions us to have in terms of our clothes, our expressions, our mannerisms. To that end, queer and feminist movements have the same enemy. These movements are supposed to be sister movements that push each other up and stand on each other's shoulders.

Justice Kaul was the only one who found the SMA to be unconstitutional. As a result, instead of adding or deleting phrases, he struck it down as being void. His reasoning was that there was a clear difference between heterosexual couples and non-heterosexual ones, but the differentiation did not meet the threshold of constitutional permissibility of such discrimination. He further held that merely facilitating interfaith marriages could not be enough intent to leave out queer marriages. Even Justice Kaul refused to read into the statute or read it down. He pointed to the 'multifarious difficulties' that would be encountered to include queer marriages within the ambit of the SMA. He took his refuge, however, in the 'limited institutional capacity' that the court had to avoid awarding marriage rights to the queer community but held that a civil union would give all rights that a marriage would.

All of us on the side of the petitioners had given the court 'workability models': Ways in which the court could have interpreted the statute to allow queer marriages within the existing framework of the SMA. The judgment does not engage effectively with any of the models or tell us why they are not workable. The engagement of the judges with the arguments of the petitioners with the cases relied on in this case leaves a lot to be desired.

The final issue was that of adoption rights. Since the book is primarily about marriage equality, and that adoption rights necessarily follow, I have not spoken of it at length. Some of the petitioners had challenged Regulation 5(3) of 2020 of the CARA guidelines. The guideline restricted the right to adopt only to single individuals and married couples who are in a 'stable marital relationship for two years'. To add to this, Section 57(2) of the Juvenile Justice (Care and Protection of Children) Act, 2015 (JJ Act) said that both 'spouses' had to consent to adoption. Additionally, there was also a CARA circular issued in 2022 which disallowed couples in live-in relationships from adopting children. The majority judgment held that it was constitutional to prohibit queer couples from adopting children. It ignored reams and reams of evidence which demonstrated that children brought up by queer persons do as well or even better than children brought up by heterosexual couples. At no point did the petitioners say that the welfare of children is not important.

Here, once again, the court ceded ground to the legislature and the executive by holding that Parliament had made the choice to only allow 'married couples' to adopt jointly. They held that this could only be achieved by the legislature, and the court could do nothing. Surprisingly, though, they acknowledged the discriminatory impact on queer couples, but yet refused to give a remedy, which would otherwise have been a logical sequitur. Even more strangely, in another classic duplicity that is characteristic of the judgment, the majority speaking through Justice Bhat notes that the 'State arguably has an even more urgent need to enable the full gamut of rights' which should be available to queer parents. He then finds that the State should 'ensure that the maximum welfare and benefits reach the largest number of children in need of safe and secure homes with a promise for their fullest development'.

The minority, however, allowed such adoptions. Justice Chandrachud, in his opinion, gave a finding that the regulation was inconsistent with the JJ Act, and thus ultra vires. Holding that the regulation violated Articles 14 and 15 of the Indian Constitution, by treating marriage as the defining criteria to adopt, he said it was discriminatory. He also noted that the Union of India had placed no data 'to support their claim that only married relationships can provide stability'.

Queer people have been adopting children as single parents and exploiting the loophole. In these cases, however, only one parent has rights over the child. What happens if the said person is unable to make decisions due to incapacity? Does this not jeopardize the welfare of the child?

Justices Bhat and Kohli's opinion, which formed the majority opinion, was a narrowly construed version of what fundamental rights jurisprudence in this country ought to be. It ignored the previous judgments of the Supreme Court, was rife with logical and legal fallacies, and set the stage for wide interference of the executive in the private lives of citizens. We had, as petitioners, argued for a fundamental right to marry, but reached at it through different legal pathways. Some arguments were rooted in dignity, some in right to family, others in impermissibility of discrimination. The argument that Anand Grover put forth was rooted in the right to intimate association. Yet, the furthest the majority went was recognizing a right to relationship which translated into a right to 'choose a partner, cohabit and enjoy physical intimacy with them, to live the way they wish to, and other rights that flow from the right to privacy, autonomy and dignity'. It also held that the right has to be protected by the State.

But still, they refused to accord sanction to the minority opinion of Justice Chandrachud which provided for guidelines for the protection of queer couples from violence by non-State actors, which I spoke about in Chapter 1. Therein lies the characteristic duplicitousness of this opinion, and the reason for this, according to the majority, was an absence of a statute. Remember, there was a statute, which could, admittedly with some degree of labour, be interpreted to include queer couples. On the other hand, he even disagreed with the minority on the right to a civil union, as the minority understood it. He said that this right could not lead to the conclusion 'the conclusion that all persons . . . have an entitlement to enter into a union, or an abiding cohabitational relationship which the state is under an obligation to recognize . . .'

On the argument that the fact that queer people were not included under the SMA, Bhat held that under-inclusion or leaving out a class of citizens from the ambit of the statute was not discriminatory. He held that 'exclusion or under-inclusion, per se, cannot be characterised as discriminatory, unless the excluded category of persons, things or matters, which are subject matter of the law (or policy) belong to the same class (the included class)'.

The second issue is in how the opinion of Justices Bhat and Kohli recognize that there is a discriminatory impact of the law on queer persons, but yet, they failed to provide a remedy. It is not as if the opinion authored by Bhat is blind to the discrimination that I have spoken of all throughout this book. He notes in paragraph 114 of the judgment that '[t]he denial of these benefits and inability of the earning partner in a queer relationship, therefore, has an adverse discriminatory impact'. If there is discrimination, then there must be a remedy. For the settled principle of law is that if the court finds that there is a violation of a right, then there must be a remedy, or *ubi jus, ibi remedium.* There is a long line of precedent of the Supreme Court itself, which holds that there must be a remedy if there is a discriminatory impact of the law on citizens, but not in today's Supreme Court. Those decisions have been, through all sorts of legal acrobatics, ignored or differentiated.

If Justice Bhat did not want to address the discrimination, he should have agreed at the very least to protection against violence, and the constitution of a high-powered committee (though I have little faith in one), which he also refused. I have spoken on this judgment at various places, and I have called it an act of judicial abstention. I must correct myself—this is an act of judicial cowardice, which is an unconscionable deed of constitutional sacrilege which will not stand the test of time and will be overruled by a future, wiser bench.

The concurring opinion of Justice Narsimha is an equally strange opinion as that of Justice Bhat. As Indira Jaising writes, this opinion was written by a—

> [J]udge here who has abandoned his judicial robe and put on that of a mystic . . . The logical fallacies and contradictions in this judgment are immense. Understating statutes is weak, with an inability to distinguish between formal validity and substantive validity of a marriage, an understanding of what are called "personal laws" is absent (notice that the words are not mentioned here). If indeed there is no fundamental right to marry, what is there to prevent the State from telling us who to marry and who not to marry, or from saying Bharatiya culture will determine that question as well?[5]

Justice Narasimha held that marriage is not a fundamental right because while the State restricts it through various ways, such as when it comes to the age of marriage and prohibited degrees, it always accommodates customs and religious usage. This accommodation, he says restricts its elevation to a fundamental right. He writes, in paragraph 12,

> In my considered opinion, the institutional space of marriage is conditioned and occupied synchronously by legislative interventions, customary practises and religious beliefs . . . Given this nature of marriage as an institution, the right to choose a spouse and the right of a consenting couple to be recognized within the institution of marriage cannot but be said to be restricted.

The only thing ignored in all of this, is the Constitution and its morality, which our Supreme Court has held is the only touchstone on which any legislation, custom, practice and belief has to be tested.[6]

Minority judgments are essential in that they often appeal to the brooding spirit of the law, in the words of Charles Evans Hughes. However, the majority and the minority seem to be in consensus here on the broad issue of a fundamental right to marry. Justice Oliver Wendell Holmes, one of the greatest judges of the US Supreme Court, once wrote:

> Great cases like hard cases make for bad law. For great cases are called great not by reason of their real importance in shaping the law of the future but because of some accident of immediate overwhelming interest which appeals to the feelings and distorts the judgment. The immediate interests exercise a kind of hydraulic pressure which makes what previously was clear seem doubtful, and before which even well-settled principles of law will bend.[7]

Nothing describes this case better. I am often asked why I think we lost. Some people say that the matter should not have been filed in the Supreme Court when it was pending before various high courts. I think this critique is unfair—even if the petitioners would not have filed for a transfer or filed fresh matters in the Supreme Court, the Union had already made a statement that it would do so before one high court. So, this critique, in my opinion, is intellectually lazy.

The second issue, I think, is that the court perhaps did not realize when it was fast-tracking this matter the amount of blowback it would receive on social media. Vicious trolling of judges, immense and improper blowback from the bar through both the Supreme Court Bar Association president Adish Aggarwala giving statements, and the Bar Council of India releasing a statement on this matter when it was sub judice may have affected the court. There was also political blowback in Parliament by speeches from members of Parliament like Sushil Kumar Modi, which saw no impropriety against an explicit bar in the rules of both houses to discuss matters which were sub judice.

Immediately after the judgment was delivered, Sriram Panchu, a senior advocate, wrote a judgement by an imaginary sixth judge in *Frontline*. Mr Panchu, in his characteristic style, took the court to the cleaners. While the whole piece deserves a read, for the purposes of this book, I only reproduce some parts of it. He illustrated the discrimination against queer lawyers like Kirpal and beacons of hope like Justice Anand Venkatesh. Panchu writes:

We have assembled here to decide a question which, to my mind, is one of the most important that we will ever be called upon to decide. The question concerns some of us most crucially and fundamentally; it concerns the rest peripherally since their lives are not subject to the outcome of our decision; it concerns all of us because it puts to test if we are really living up to the basic tenets of humaneness and democracy and our fundamental and primordial values . . . None of us sitting in judgment over the world of the petitioners before us has the slightest inkling of the nature of that world. These are persons with a sexual orientation different from the majority of society. Their orientation is towards persons of the same sex. That is the only difference. Beyond that, the feelings they have, the affection, love, care, the wanting to be together and share life with another mirror that which the rest of us aspire to. The love for another, the central love for a soulmate is the core intrinsic basic part of our being. All of us know that, have felt it, experienced it, and it has enriched our lives immeasurably. Our happiness is the derivative of that; shorn of that, life is a lonely tracking through our brief existence in this world. And the ones who feel the loneliness the most are the ones from whom the partner is snatched away. By Death, the Grim Reaper, usually. And occasionally Human Hands, which take away not the partner but the partnership; as terrible, if not worse. What know we of their world? Nothing. We may have heard about a relative or a friend, but it is a matter that stays within whispers in close family circles, such is the shame that society has fashioned on it. Times are changing fast, but one essential attribute of the judicial process is that its grandmasters are steeped in tradition, convention and precedent; that is how their world works, and their world rules their minds . . . I hope these young men and women whose hopes have been dimmed, if not dashed, by this judgment of ours, plant a tree on this spot. I hope this tree grows quickly with luxuriant foliage and dwarfs the building opposite. And I hope that one day a Constitutional Court will direct the doors facing it to be opened to let in fresh light and air and the view beyond. They will see the tree. And between them and the tree is the statue of Mahatma Gandhi, to mediate between law and society. And hopefully, someone in the Court will recall what the Mahatma said: 'Whenever you are in doubt, or when the self becomes too much with you, apply the following test. Recall the face of the poorest and the weakest man you may have seen, and ask yourself, if the step you contemplate is going to be of any use to him.' I rest now. Not in peace but with hope. The hope that Justice will ultimately trump Law. It usually does.[8]

This judgment will not stand long. In the history of the Supreme Court of our country, there times when the court has faltered. Some of these discordant notes have been cases like A.K. Gopalan v. State of Madras,[9] which held that Article 21 did not recognize the right to due process, ADM Jabalpur v. Shivkant Shukla,[10] which held that a right to personal liberty can be suspended in the larger interest of the State, and, of course, the recriminalization of homosexuality in *Koushal*.[11] Each of these decisions has been considered a stain on the Supreme Court and its legacy. Eventually, sooner rather than later, these decisions have been overturned. While overruling *ADM Jabalpur*, Justice Sanjay Kishan Kaul held, 'I fully agree with the view expressly overruling the ADM Jabalpur case which was an aberration in the constitutional jurisprudence of our country and the desirability of burying the majority opinion ten fathoms deep, with no chance of resurrection.' I believe that sooner rather than later *Supriyo* will meet the same fate: in future, I have no doubt that a wiser bench will also hold that the majority opinion in Supriyo should be buried ten fathoms deep, with no chance of resurrection.

After the judgment, I remember having multiple breakdowns. It felt like a deep personal failure. To this day, I cannot speak or write about the judgment without my eyes welling up. To say that this has been one of the greatest failures of my life at a professional level would not be wrong. But reviews had to be drafted, and there was little time for wallowing in self-pity. All of us drafted and filed review petitions over the thirty days following the judgment. In essence, the gist of the review was best captured by Udit Sood's review petition which said, 'To find that the petitioners are enduring discrimination, but then turn them away with best wishes for the future, conforms neither with this Hon'ble Court's Constitutional obligation towards queer Indians nor with the separation of powers contemplated in our Constitution.' This was a divergence from the classic style of drafting legal petitions. While drafting, lawyers are taught to stay away from adjectives, epithets and hyperbole. 'Keep it short and simple, stupid' is something which is drilled into us during our legal training. Yet it was clear that it was the deep pain of the petitioners which was coming forth in the draft.

The matters were mentioned before the Chief Justice on 23 November 2023. Chief Justice Chandrachud agreed to consider whether the review petitions should be heard in open court on 28 November. As a matter of course, review petitions are not heard in open court. On 28 November when the cause list came out, the matter was not on board for reasons best known to the Chief Justice who has the power to decide when and who should hear matters. Review petitions are often not taken up for months, if not years. A review petition is heard by the same bench, so we mentioned them with a solemn hope that the review could be heard before Justice Kaul, who had written the most radically liberal opinion of the bench (which still did not give marriage but civil unions and struck down the SMA), and that he would be on the bench for the review. Alas, that was not to be, and Justice Kaul retired before the issue of whether the review petition would be heard in open court was decided. Subsequently, a new bench consisting of Justices Sanjeev Khanna and B.V. Nagarathana in place of Justices Bhat and Kaul who had superannuated was constituted. However, Justice Khanna recused himself from the matter, and we now await the constitution of yet another bench. The matter will be taken up sooner rather than later. We now have the benefit of hindsight to figure out where we went wrong and do better in the future for not just the marriage equality movement, but also the broader movement of queer rights in general.

But merely resting easy with filing reviews for this judgment is not enough. The goal for those of us who are a part of the movement is also to chart a future course and a manifesto. Such a manifesto ought to be drawn by the movement—but what I want to do here is talk about the issues which will undoubtedly come up in the future or are already being fought for inside and outside the courts. These issues are not urban or elite but are the truths of the lives of hundreds of thousands of queer people in the country. The way that queer lives intersect with the heterosexual world, in their social, legal, economic and overall manifestations, is far from perfect.

We must continue fighting for individual rights, in addition to the broader fight for equality. For love is not enough to give us a human existence unless we have rights that are firmly grounded. Consider, for example, the case which came up before the Kerala High Court. It involved claims over the dead body of a gay man who died while living with his partner. He was disowned by his family, and they did not want to claim the body. The partner had no legal rights over his body. In this situation, it is for the state to dispose of the body as it was legally unclaimed. No matter how much the two partners loved each other, there were no precipitative rights. What do we do with a right to relationship that Bhat talks about? It gives us the square root of nothing. The Kerala High Court held that the family who had refused the body earlier and did not pay for the hospital expenditure had a right over the body and chose to hand it to them while the lover had merely been left out in the cold winds of exclusion and homophobia. To be queer in a way that the law does not recognize your relationship, and the courts, while sympathizing with the lack of recognition but providing no redress, will rob queer people of their dignity in life and in death. It will take this case and several gut-wrenching cases like it for us to build up a solid substratum for marriage equality in the future. But one thing is certain, no matter how many judicial platitudes say otherwise, in India, queer people are second-class citizens. Except, unlike in *Koushal*, this time the judgment employs woke language in denying us our rights.

How, then, does one chart the way forward? How do we ensure that there is a way ahead for the queer movement in the midst of divisions that are rife within the community—some for good reason? The answer to this would be charting a manifesto that deals with not just the times we live in but is more inclusive in its formulation and conceptualization. Of course, as I have said repeatedly in this book, the work of movement-building is on building solidarities, and that must start within the queer movement itself. A manifesto such as this should be based on consultation within the community across the country. There are deep wounds in the community—caste-based discrimination, the growing distance between cis and trans movements, and differences across other intersectionalities such as religion, class, disability and race.

In the run-up to the 2024 general elections, three parties, the Indian National Congress, the Communist Party of India (Marxist) and the Communist Party of India (Marxist–Leninist) gave explicit promises on queer relationships. The Congress promised to enact a law for civil unions for queer couples, and an amendment to Article 15 to prohibit discrimination on the grounds of sexual orientation. The CPI (M) promised a law on civil unions, an anti-discrimination bill to take measures to address bullying, violence and harassment, address ragging based on sexual orientation and gender, gender-neutral bathrooms and horizontal reservations in public education. The CPI (ML) manifesto went further and included promises to guarantee the constitutional rights of the transgender community including all necessary protections and welfare measures mandated by the NALSA judgment. The manifesto further promised adequate legal protection and support mechanisms for LGBTQIA+ persons and assured that the party would pass a legislation recognizing the right of any two persons to enter into a civil union without discrimination on sexual orientation and gender identity. Even the BJP was shocked into action and formed a committee as per the Supreme Court guidelines, consisting only of government secretaries and having a much narrower remit than what the court directed.

There is no denying that we live in strange times. The broader politics of the country has seen a clampdown on civil liberties, and an attack on civil society. As a result, queer rights have also come under assault: Bans on begging for transgender persons, despite begging not being a crime, permissions denied for pride marches, and the wider ills of a homo-nationalist undercurrent which runs within the movement. There are systemic attacks on the Constitution, on democracy and democratic values, on institutional integrity, on liberty and secularism. If the queer movement falls prey to such tropes that exclude, then we lose all rights to call ourselves an inclusive movement. The queer movement should give as much space for a queer Kashmiri Muslim or a Dalit queer person as it does for an upper-caste, upper-class gay man from Delhi. We are far from there. We must be loyal to constitutional values if we are going to use the power of the Constitution to seek equality for ourselves. The exclusion and oppression from within must stop. The issues of horizontal reservations for transgender persons, an anti-discrimination law, seeking affirmative and affordable medical treatment for queer persons, bans on conversion therapy, dealing with bullying and abuse in online and offline spaces are some of the issues that are rife in the community. A single-axis framework that deals with oppression helps no one, and it is essential that we chart a manifesto for New India, and in Amrit Kaal in a way that is truly inclusive. While the petitions for horizontal reservations, anti-bullying guidelines and challenges to the Trans Act are pending before various high courts and the Supreme Court, we do not see a fraction of media attention given to these petitions. You cannot make anti-discrimination as sexy or as Instagram-able as you can make marriages. But these are perhaps more urgent issues that we must deal with with equal alacrity and alarm as this case, if not more. The times ahead are dire, and the Supreme Court has collapsed for all purposes, and the protection of civil liberties is at its nadir.

What happens now? We continue to be resilient, and we continue to be hopeful. But more importantly, we continue to love, rage and spread queer euphoria. We stop being polite citizens. We connect to our roots, make a stronger claim for liberation. Our resistance must be ecstatic. Our resistance must be determined. But most importantly, we must continue to keep faith and do everything in our power to ensure that democracy and democratic institutions are strengthened. We must continue the hard work of movement-building, because if there is no hope in the Supreme Court and the Constitution itself to fulfil constitutional promises and protect the citizenry from executive excesses and legislative discrimination, where will the citizenry go? Or as the biblical adage goes, if the salt hath lost its savour, wherewith shall it be salted?

Acknowledgements

Any such project would not have been possible without accruing personal, professional and intellectual debts. The people I mention here are only a few in the long list of names who have encouraged me, been my cheerleaders and helped me in finishing the book:

First, Ms Indira Jaising, who took me on as a fledgling young lawyer fresh out of grad school, and who taught me all that I know about the law, and Mr Anand Grover, who led me in this case, suffered my anxieties and impertinences, and allowed me the space to propose arguments throughout the drafting and arguing of the case. Paras Nath Singh taught me things that one does not learn in law school, from curing defects in petitions to ensuring that the documents are properly proofread. He has also been a steadfast friend. Sadeeq-Ur-Rahman, the perianal source of mirth in the office has been a true friend.

Secondly, Professor Michele B. Goodwin, who told me that I had something important to say and taught me to believe in my own words. Without her encouragement, I would never have put out in the world any part of this book or any other piece of writing.

Aryan Soni and Maitrey Prajapati, my oldest and best friends, who have been there for me come hell or high water.

When I moved from Mumbai to Delhi, there were people who made Delhi home. To Shivangi Sharma and Pragya Jain, who let me be their de facto house cat for nearly a year. Rahul Sangwan, Aryan D'Rozario, Samarth Malhotra, Sankalp Inugati, Saurabh Kirpal, Nicholas Bacchman, Sharif Rangnekar, Vaivab Das, Alexander Balakrishnan, Moksh Kalra, Jwalin Patel, Luke Butcher, Shilpa Rao, Shivangi Sharma and countless others, who have been home away from home and have been steadfast in their support for me not just in this book, but in life as well. It is kindness of friends like this that makes surviving in this city possible.

My law school friends, who were often the ray of hope in the dark recesses of the closet: Anjana, Vishesh, Samidha, Kartik, Ritik and others.

Chaitanya, who dealt with an immensely (and dare I say, equally) whack person during the writing of this book. He stuck by my side and added mirth when life seemed dark.

Anish Gawande is someone I turn to for both the smallest of things and big life decisions. From not letting me buy a fountain in the shape of a dog to helping me deal with life crises, he has been a true friend whenever he replies to messages or answers a phone call.

Kanmani R., Vyjayanti Vasanta Mogli, Santa Khurrai and countless other queer and trans persons on whose shoulders I stand. I have benefited and learnt from the compassion that they bring to their work and activism.

Kanishka Gupta, who believed in me when I first sent him my proposal for a different book and decided to take on a hitherto unknown writer. He has been an extremely generous agent, with his patience as well as his words.

Narayani Basu, who edited the proposal and the first chapter, has been a guiding light for me in the world of publishing, which I knew little about. She will always be my favourite editor, for few people have spoken to me as gently but plainly as she has.

This book would not have been possible without incisive comments by Mihir Rajamane, Arif Ayaz Parrey and Jaideep Singh Lalli. Mihir has gone through multiple iterations of this book, providing substantive and editorial feedback. Suffice to say, this book would have been impossible without him. Arif went out of his way and provided me with comments despite being ill, and Jaideep battled great personal loss but remained a steadfast friend and critic.

Of course, I owe a debt of gratitude to the lovely folks at Penguin: Chirag Thakkar, who commissioned this by randomly sliding into my DMs one day, has turned into a close friend; Anushree Kaushal, who has indefatigably worked on the manuscript and provided me with extensive comments on the book to turn it into something that is more structurally sound; Gurveen Chadha, who has been patient and kind, yet laser-focused on the deadline and getting the book out on time. I would also like to thank Aparna Abhijit for bearing with my idiosyncrasies throughout the typesetting process, and Prateek Agarwal for handling the marketing of the book. Sparsh Raj Singh also deserves a shout-out for keeping up with my never-ending demands about the cover design.

Finally, my family, who have always stood strong by me and have had tremendous faith, not just in my abilities but also the fact that I will make trouble for myself, which I have continued to do since childhood: Dad, my superhero; Mum, who instilled a love for books in me, is my favourite person in the whole wide world; and Panistha, who has been the de facto research assistant for this book, and toiled tirelessly over the documents and data that I asked her to.

Notes

Chapter 1: Queer Revolutions: The Personal, the Political and the Legal

1 Select portions of this chapter appeared in the Leaflet on 6 September 2022.

2 Suresh Kumar Koushal v. Naz Foundation, (2014) 1 SCC 1.

3 Naz Foundation v. State (NCT of Delhi), 2009 SCC OnLine Del 1762.

4 Supriyo Chakraborty v. Union of India, 2023 SCC OnLine SC 1348.

5 Afeeza Fathima, 'Union Govt Did Not Publicise Section 377 Judgement despite Court Order, RTIs Reveal', NewsMinute, 19 April 2023, https://www.thenewsminute. com/news/union-govt-did-not-publicise-section-377-judgement-despite-court-order-rtis-reveal-176090.

6 Saba Naqvi, 'Women's Reservation: A Law on Paper, but a Reality Far Away', Frontline, 3 October 2023, https:// frontline.thehindu.com/politics/womens-reservation-a-law-on-paper-but-a-reality-far-away-saba-naqvi-nari-shakti-vandan-adhiniyam-women-in-parliament-state-assembly/ article67345156.ece.

7 The Telangana Eunuchs Act was struck down by a division bench of the Telangana High Court by Chief Justice Ujjal

Bhuyan (as he then was) and C. V. Bhaskara Reddy on a PIL in Vyjayanti Vasantha Mogli v. State of Telangana, Writ Petition (PIL) No. 44 and 355 of 2018, and 74 of 2020.

8   The only exceptions to this are the two major cases, the Fourth Judges Case (Supreme Court Advocates on Record Association v. Union of India, [2015] 13 SCR 1), where the Supreme Court struck down the Constitution (Ninety-Ninth Amendment) Act, 2014 (99th Amendment), along with the National Judicial Appointments Commission Act, 2014 (NJAC Act), which gave the executive a primacy in matters of judicial appointments, and the electoral bonds case, where the Supreme Court held that the Electoral Bonds Scheme denied the voter the right to information (Association for Democratic Reforms v. Union of India, 2024 INSC 113).

9   Indira Jaising, '2023: The Year of the Suraj Mukhi Court', Leaflet, 2 January 2024, https://theleaflet.in/2023-the-year-of-the-surajmukhi-court/.

10 Oliver Wendell Holmes, *The Common Law* (American Bar Association, 2009).

11 Supriyo Chakraborty v. Union of India, 2023 INSC 920.

12 Oishik Sircar and Dipika Jain, eds, *New Intimacies, Old Desires: Law, Culture and Queer Politics in Neoliberal Times* (Delhi: Zubaan, 2017).

13 Rohit De, *A People's Constitution: The Everyday Life of Law in the Indian Republic* (Princeton University Press, 2018).

14 Gautam Bhatia, 'Coronavirus and the Constitution—XXXV: Dialogic Judicial Review in the Supreme Court', *Indian Constitutional Law and Philosophy*, 28 April 2021, https://indconlawphil.wordpress.com/2021/04/28/coronavirus-and-the-constitution-xxxv-dialogic-judicial-review-in-the-supreme-court/.

15 John P. Mullooly, 'The Price of Liberty Is Eternal Vigilance', Linacre Quarterly 9 (1988) 55, http://journals.sagepub.com/doi/10.1080/00243639.1988.11877948, accessed 8 April 2024.

16 *Indian Express*, 'Gujarat Confidential: Amid Legal Battle over Same-Sex Marriage, a Pride Scarf at Law University Convocation', 5 April 2023, *https://indianexpress.com/article/cities/ahmedabad/gujarat-confidential-pride-scarf-bjp-8539513*, accessed 12 April 2024.

17 Rohin Bhatt, 'As a Queer Person and a Lawyer, I Believe It Is Illegal to Deny Same-Sex Couples the Right to Marry', *Indian Express*, 25 March 2023, https://indianexpress.com/article/opinion/columns/queer-person-lawyer-illegal-deny-same-sex-couples-right-marry-8518410/.

18 Tahir Mahmood, 'Tahir Mahmood on Same-Sex Marriage: Existing Matrimonial Law Should Be Left Exclusively for the "Sanskaar" Called "Marriage"', *Indian Express*, 22 March 2023, https://indianexpress.com/article/opinion/columns/sex-marriage-matrimonial-law-should-be-left-exclusively-for-marriage-8512611/, accessed 12 April 2024.

19 G.S. Bajpai and Ankit Kaushik, 'Same-Sex Marriages: A Matter for Parliament', *The Hindu*, 2 April 2023, https://www.thehindu.com/opinion/op-ed/same-sex-marriages-a-matter-for-parliament/article66692014.ece.

20 Rohin Bhatt, 'A Case for Marriage Equality', *The Hindu*, 5 April 2023, https://www.thehindu.com/opinion/op-ed/a-case-for-marriage-equality/article66698340.ece.

21 Proverbs 1:2–6, English Standard Version, Crossway Bibles (ed.), *ESV: Study Bible: English Standard Version* (ESV text ed., Crossway Bibles 2007).

Chapter 2: A Judicial Punch in the Gut and the Way Forward

1   Larry Mitchell, *The Faggots and Their Friends Between Revolutions* (New York: Calamus Books, 1977).

2   ADM Jabalpul v. Shivkant Shukla.

3   Tanya Arora, 'Equal marriage rights: those for and those against, a review', Center for Justice and Peace, 2 May 2023, https://cjp.org.in/equal-marriage-rights-those-for-and-those-against-a-review/.

4   Rohin Bhatt, 'Death by suicide of a 16-year-old queer person: Why don't you care when we are bullied? Death by suicide of a 16-year-old queer person: Why don't you care when we are bullied?', *Indian Express*, 29 November 2023, https://indianexpress.com/article/opinion/death-by-suicide-of-a-16-year-old-queer-person-the-politics-of-palatability-and-the-failure-to-protect-children-9044073/.

5   Larry Mitchell, *The Faggots and Their Friends Between Revolutions* (New York: Calamus Books, 1977).

6   Kenneth W. Mack, 'Rethinking Civil Rights Lawyering and Politics in the Era before Brown', *Yale Law Journal* 115 (2005): 256, 258.

7   Section 16 of the Advocates Act, 1961.

8   Indira Jaising v. Supreme Court of India, (2017) 9 SCC 766.

9   Utkarsh Anand, '11 Women, 34 First-Gen Lawyers among 56 Designated as "Senior Advocates" by SC', *Hindustan Times*, 19 January 2024. https://www.hindustantimes.com/india-news/11-women-34-first-gen-lawyers-among-56-designated-as-senior-advocates-by-sc-101705687170296.html.

10 Christopher W. Schmidt, 'Divided by Law: The Sit-Ins and the Role of the Courts in the Civil Rights

Movement', *Law and History Review* 33 (2015): 93, https://www.cambridge.org/core/product/identifier/ S0738248014000509/type/journal_article, accessed 21 January 2024.

11   Mark Tushnet, 'The Critique of Rights', *SMU Law Review* 47: 23, https://scholar.smu.edu/cgi/viewcontent. cgi?article=2336&context=smulr#:~:text=The%20 critique%20of%20rights%20is,of%20the%20work%20 they%20do.

12   Shreshtha Das and Ahmad Bund, 'The Homonationalist Agenda of "Good" Queers Who Love the Nation-State', Wire, 13 February 2020, https://thewire.in/lgbtqia/ homonationalism-india-sedition.

13   Dr Jaya Thakur v. Union of India, Writ Petition (Civil) 1000/2022.

14   Das and Bund, 'The Homonationalist Agenda of 'Good' Queers Who Love the Nation-State'.

15   Abhijit Iyer-Mitra, 'Fighting 377, Stupidly: In Seeking 15 Seconds of Fame, Gay Rights Activists Have Only Lost Valuable Time', Daily O, 12 July 2018, https://www. dailyo.in/politics/fighting-377%E2%80%93stupidly- in-seeking-15%E2%80%93seconds-of-fame-gayrights- activists-have-only-lost-valuable-time-25427.

16   Kimberley Crenshaw, 'Mapping the Margins: Intersectionality, Identity Politics, and Violence against Women of Color', *Stanford Law Review* 43, no. 6 (1991): 1241–99.

17   Dhiren Borisa, 'Hopeful Rantings of a Dalit-Queer Person', *JLHR* (Jindal Law and Humanities Review? 1 (2020): 91.

18   Manu Sebastian, 'Supreme Court's "Illegal but Permissible" Jurisprudence', Live Law, 30 July 2023.

19   Supreme Court Advocates-on-Record Assn v. Union of India, (2016) 5 SCC 1.

20   Assn for Democratic Reforms v. Union of India, (2024) 243 Comp Cas 115.

21   William O. Douglas, *America Challenged* 4–5 (1960).

22   'The SPIT Manifesto', https://static1.squarespace.com/static/5d40a0bea6305d0001bc1663/t/5e71ae76539f80 0fe98afc3f/1584508595297/SPIT%21Reader-2017.pdf.

Chapter 3: The Judicial Journey

1   Marsha P. Johnson and Sylvia Rivera, *Street Transvestite Action Revolutionaries: Survival, Revolt and Queer Antagonist Struggle* (Untorelli Press, 2013).

2   Queen Empress v. Khairati, (1884) ILR 6 All 204.

3   Oishik Sircar and Dipika Jain, 'Of Powerful Feelings and Facile Gestures', in *New Intimacies, Old Desires: Law, Culture and Queer Politics in Neoliberal Times*, eds Oishik Sircar and Dipika Jain, (2017), p. xiv.

4   'Less than Gay', https://docs.google.com/file/d/0BwDli puQ0I6ZMXVmNWk0ajdqWEU/edit?resourcekey=0-BCJz6nCJeIVOg5_mTcG9cA.

5   Kajal Bhardwaj, 'Reforming Macaulay', 2 July 2012, https://orinam.net/reforming-macaulay.

6   Justice Leila Seth, 'A Mother and a Judge Speaks out on Section 377', *Times of India*, 26 January 2014, https://timesofindia.indiatimes.com/home/sunday-times/deep-focus/a-mother-and-a-judge-speaks-out-on-section-377/articleshow/29383723.cms, accessed 12 February 2024.

7   Danish Sheikh, 'A Summary of the 15th April 2014 Judgement of NALSA v. Union of India', https://orinam.net/content/wp-content/uploads/2014/04/nalsa_summary_danish.pdf.

8 Paragraph 109.

9 M.P. Sharma v. Satish Chandra, (1954) 1 SCC 385.

10 Kharak Singh v. State of U.P., (1964) 1 SCR 332.

11 Supreme Court Observer, 'Judgment of the Court in Plain English (I)', 24 August 2017, https://www. scobserver.in/reports/k-s-puttaswamy-right-to-privacy-judgment-of-the-court-in-plain-english-i/.

12 Print, '"I Believe What I Wrote Should Be the Law on Article 370", Former Supreme Court Judge Justice Sanjay K. Kaul', YouTube interview, 26 December 2023, https:// www.youtube.com/watch?v=Gd6y0kSe8mk&t=686s.

13 Vqueeram Aditya Sahai and Akhil Kang, 'Guruswamy and Katju, Your Rainbow Doesn't Hide Your Casteism', *Akademi Magazine*, 2020.

14 Azeefa Fathima and Sukanya Shaji, 'Union Govt Did Not Publicise Section 377 Judgement Despite Court Order, RTIs Reveal'. *News Minute*, 19 April 2023, https://www.thenewsminute.com/news/union-govt-did-not-publicise-section-377-judgement-despite-court-order-rtis-reveal-176090, accessed 12 February 2024.

Chapter 4: Acerbity, Acrimony and Arguments

1 Larry Mitchell, The Faggots and Their Friends Between Revolutions (New York: Calamus Books, 1977).

2 Leaflet, 'LGBTQ+: Petition for Marriage Equality Filed in Kerala High Court', 29 January 2020, https:// theleaflet.in/lgbtq-petition-for-marriage-equality-filed-in-kerala-high-court-2.

3 *Indian Express*, 'Live Streaming of Same-Sex Marriages Case: Delhi High Court Takes Exception to Centre's Affidavit, 17 May 2022, https://indianexpress. com/article/cities/delhi/live-streaming-of-same-sex-

marriages-delhi-high-court-takes-exception-to-centres-affidavit-7921898.

4   Anuj Garg v. Hotel Assn of India, (2008) 3 SCC 1.

5   Air India v. Nargesh Meerza, (1981) 4 SCC 335.

6   Simone de Beauvoir, *The Second Sex*, trans. Constance Capisto-Borde and Sheila Malovany-Chevallier (Vintage Books, 2011).

7   Benoit Denizet-Lewis, 'Young Gay Rites', 27 April 2008, *New York Times*, http://www.nytimes.com/2008/04/27/magazine/27young-t.html?scp1/41&sq1/4Denizet-Lewis%20Young%20Gay%20Rites&st1/4cse.

8   Lawrence v. Texas, 539 U.S. 558.

9   Sheyril Agarwal, Joyojeet Pal and Tanishka Sodhi, 'Anti-Hindu, Woke Feminist: Inside the Unprecedented Online Trolling of CJI Chandrachud', Newslaundry, 30 May 2023, https://www.newslaundry.com/2023/05/30/anti-hindu-woke-feminist-inside-the-unprecedented-online-trolling-of-cji-chandrachud, accessed 12 February 2024.

10 Supra.

11 Kesavananda Bharati v. State of Kerala, (1973) 4 SCC 225.

12 K.S. Puttaswamy (Privacy-9J.) v. Union of India, (2017) 10 SCC 1.

13 Shakti Vahini v. Union of India, (2018) 7 SCC 192.

14 Shafin Jahan v. Asokan K.M., (2018) 16 SCC 368.

15 Laxmibai Chandaragi B. v. State of Karnataka, (2021) 3 SCC 360.

16 Shafin Jahan v. Asokan K.M., (2018) 16 SCC 368.

17 Dobbs v. Jackson Women's Health Organization, No. 19-1392, 597 U.S.__.

18 Roe v. Wade, 410 U.S. 113 (1973).

19 Alexander Hamilton, *The Federalist Papers* (New York: Dutton/Signet, 2012).

20 Worcester v. Georgia, 31 U.S. (6 Pet.) 515 (1832).

21 Under our system of laws, every statute provides the government to make administrative provisions in the form of rules, regulations, orders etc. to give effect to the law. The statute is called the parent act, and the rules made under it are called the delegated legislation or secondary legislation.

22 Deepika Singh v. Central Administrative Tribunal, 2022 SCC OnLine SC 1088.

23 Ghaidan v. Godin-Mendoza [2004] UKHL 30.

24 Oscar Wilde, *The Picture of Dorian Gray* (London: Penguin, 2003).

25 State v. Jagdish B. Rau, 1969 SCC OnLine Bom 62.

26 Randhir Singh v. Union of India, (1982) 1 SCC 618.

27 Loving v. Virginia, 388 U.S. 1 (1967).

28 John Stuart Mill, *On Liberty* (NY: Dover Publications, 2002).

29 Shakti Vahini v. Union of India, (2018) 7 SCC 192.

30 *Indian Express*, 'Paratha Not Chapati, Pay 18% GST If You Can't Have Cheaper Roti', 14 October 2022, https://indianexpress.com/article/business/economy/paratha-not-chapati-pay-18-gst-if-you-cant-have-cheaper-roti-8207454/.

31 Saptarshi Mandal, 'Can Judges Deliver Marriage Equality?' Law and Other Things, 13 March 2023, https://lawandotherthings.com/can-judges-deliver-marriage-equality.

32 X v. State (NCT of Delhi), (2023) 9 SCC 433.

Chapter 5: Macabre and Malice

1 Larry Mitchell, *The Faggots and Their Friends Between Revolutions* (New York: Calamus Books, 1977).
2 William Shakespeare, *Julius Caesar* (New York: Dover Publications, 1991).
3 Case of Schlak and Kopf v. Austria (Application no. 30141/04).
4 United Nations Office of High Commission for Human Rights, Frequently Asked Questions on Economic, Social and Cultural Rights, Fact Sheet Number 33, available at: https://www.ohchr.org/sites/default/files/Documents/Issues/ESCR/FAQ_on_ESCR-en.pdf.>.
5 Masterpiece Cakeshop, Ltd., et al v. Colorado Civil Rights Commission, et al., 584 U.S. 617 (2018).

Chapter 6: The Return Fire

1 Oscar Wilde, *The Picture of Dorian Gray* (London: Penguin, 2003).
2 'Convention on the Elimination of All Forms of Discrimination against Women', *Treaty Series*, United Nations (1988), 1249: 13.
3 James Kirkup, 'The Love that Dares to Speak Its Name', UNC Libraries, https://exhibits.lib.unc.edu/items/show/6190.

Chapter 7: Excluded but Not Condemned: The Judgment and the Way Ahead

1 Arunkumar v. Inspector General of Registration, 2019 SCC OnLine Mad 8779.

2 Vishaka v. State of Rajasthan, (1997) 6 SCC 241.

3 Anoop Baranwal v. Union of India [Election Commission Appointments], (2023) 6 SCC 161.

4 S. Shilpa Sailesh v. Varun Sreenivasan, 2023 SCC OnLine SC 544.

5 Indira Jaising, 'From the Certainty of the Constitution towards Amorphous Culture and Customs', Wire, 6 January 2024, https://thewire.in/law/marriage-equality-narasimha-supreme-court-cji-chandrachud.

6 Indian Young Lawyers Assn (Sabarimala Temple-5J.) v. State of Kerala, (2019) 11 SCC 1.

7 Northern Securities Co. v. United States, 193 U.S. 197 (1904).

8 Sriram Panchu, 'In the Supreme Court of Erewhon: The Unseen Sixth Judge Renders His Verdict in Supriyo v. Union of India', Frontline, 26 October 2023, https://frontline.thehindu.com/the-nation/satire-supreme-court-of-erewhon-unseen-judge-opines-on-marriage-equality/article67461218.ece.

9 A.K. Gopalan v. State of Madras, 1950 SCC 228.

10 ADM, Jabalpur v. Shivkant Shukla, (1976) 2 SCC 521.

11 Suresh Kumar Koushal v. Naz Foundation, (2014) 1 SCC 1.

Scan QR code to access the
Penguin Random House India website